CREATIONS 2020

CREATIONS 2020

Ada Writers

Creations 2020 is a mix of fiction and nonfiction by respective authors. Names, place, and incidents may be products of the authors imagination or the writer's interpretation. Any resemblance to actual events, locals, businesses, or any persons, living or dead, to include the re-telling through the author's eyes are considered coincidental.

ISBN-13:9798673863206

DEDICATION

This book is dedicated to our friend and fellow Ada Writer, Anita Robertson. Her bubbly personality and wacky humor keep us smiling. Her artistic abilities keep us in awe. Her friendship warms our hearts. Anita, thank you for volunteering your talents to edit this book. We would be lost without you, Comma Queen!

ACKNOWLEDGMENTS

Thank you to all who read our book.

We hope you enjoy our stories and poems, as we have enjoyed writing them.

A special thank you to Janet McCoy of McCoy-Callison Photography in Ada, Oklahoma, who took the author portraits. Thank you for making us look good despite what you had to work with. You are indeed a miracle worker.

Thank you to the Ada Library who provided meeting space for the Ada Writers for many years until this year's Coronavirus pandemic forced the shutdown of our country and their doors.

Thank you to the Pontotoc County Technology Center, who welcomed us with open arms and provided us a new home.

Thank you to our families who love us, support us, and encourage us. Listen to our stories and always act interested. We love you!

ABOUT OUR COVER

Our cover photo was taken by Ada Writer's own, Betty Crow.

It depicts the natural beauty of the sunset in Ada, Oklahoma.

In addition to writing and photography, Betty enjoys, drawing and painting. Her talents amaze us. Thank you, Betty.

Table of Contents

ABOUT DEBBIE ANDERSON

Debbie Anderson, author of the mystery *Friend or Foe* is a long-time storyteller and writer. Mysteries and thrillers are her genre of choice with a little humor thrown in for good measure.

While attending Tarrant County College she took courses in Art and Design, and Creative Writing. Debbie also took classes at the Institute of Children's Literature and the University of Phoenix, graduating with a degree in Management.

She has been published in various anthologies including, Reflections (1973), Creations 2017, Creations 2018, Creations 2019, Prosateurs Tales and Truth (2018), and Prosateurs Yule Tidings (2019). She is a member of the Oklahoma Writers Federation, Inc., Writing for Fun, Prosateurs, and Ada Writers of whom she is the current president.

She once told her father she wanted to be an *arthur* when she grew up. He told her it was too late to be an *Arthur* but she could probably be an *author.*

Writing was a hobby which soon turned into a passion. After surviving two bouts of cancer, one of her many doctors suggested she should write a book. So, she did. *Friend or Foe* was published in 2018. The sequel, *Predators Among Us*, is soon to be released, as is *Lizzy*, a story for 'tweens, and *Bloodless*, a memoir of her struggle with leukemia.

She has three children, Josh, Janie, and Nathan, and four grandchildren, Austin, Sidney, Emerson, and Leila, none of whom live nearby. She is the oldest of eight children and warns her family they may appear as subjects in her books. They have provided her with years of material to work with.

She hopes you enjoy her contributions to this book.

A Flight to Remember

by Debbie Anderson

Cozumel, here we come! American Airlines decided to stop flying to this island destination, making this the last flight. As employees, my friends and I decided to take the opportunity for a girls' trip.

One by one, we checked in for the flight. The gate area permeated excitement. This wasn't a business flight. The passengers were flying for fun. Warm sunny beaches and turquoise water awaited us.

The five of us were used to packing light. After all, we flew stand-by. Chances are the plane would be full, and we couldn't travel. Or a last-minute surge of passengers, who had been waiting for their flight in the airport bar, would cause us to be bumped from the flight. We learned early on to pack only a carry-on bag. Anything checked could end up somewhere without us.

The gate agent called us to the desk.

“The flight from Dallas to Cancun is wide open, but the Cancun to Cozumel leg is pretty full.” (Airline jargon meaning there were seats available as far as Cancun, but once more passengers joined the flight in Cancun, we may be asked to deboard.)

We looked at each other and decided to take the chance. There were inexpensive shuttle flights from Cancun to Cozumel we could take if we had to.

The other passengers on the plane talked excitedly. Most wore casual clothes appropriate for a beach excursion. As airline personnel, we wore dresses with pantyhose, the required attire. We were representing American Airlines after all.

The flight was smooth and uneventful. The sun glittered in the azure sky. Even the clouds were light and wispy.

“I’ve never heard of anyone being taken off a flight once they are boarded and, in the air, have you?” Deanna asked.

“Never! I’ve seen them ask people to deboard before the flight when paying passengers show up late. But not after the flight takes off,” replied Jacqueline.

“Yeah, but she said the flight was tight from Cancun.” Deanna continued.

“I’m sure many of these passengers will be deplaning in

Cancun. How many could possibly be boarding to Cozumel?"

I sat by quietly listening to the conversation. Like Deanna, the possibility nagged me. *What will we do if we get bumped?*

"Even if the worst happens and we have to get off in Cancun, we will just catch the shuttle. It's only $38.00 one way," Jacqueline assured us.

I decided not to worry. She was probably right. Surely some of the other passengers were just going as far as Cancun.

We laughed and talked, excited with anticipation. Jacqueline and her sister Karen were the hosts of this trip. previously been scuba diving off the island and as such, they made the plans. They also carried dive masks and other gear along with their bikinis and shorts.

The plane descended to Cancun. We watched through the plane's small window as the turquoise water came closer. We were almost there.

A few people departed as the rest of us waited on the plane for any new passengers. We held our breath.

The flight attendant called us to the front of the plane where a gate agent waited.

"I'm sorry," she began, "The flight is full. Two of you will have to get off."

Deanna and I decided to stay behind to catch the shuttle. Jacqueline told us the name of the hotel where we should meet them when we arrived. "Don't worry. You won't be far behind us. It's just a ten-minute flight from here," Jacqueline assured us.

Deanna and I grabbed our bags and deboarded the plane. We found the Aero Mexico ticket counter and bought our tickets.

"Do you have any luggage?"

"Just carry-ons," I assured him.

"You'll have to check it. The plane doesn't have an overhead compartment, and there will not be enough room under the seat."

The gate agent pointed to a waiting area. "The plane will leave from that gate. Take a seat. They'll announce it when it's time to board."

"What time does the flight take off?" I asked.

"It's scheduled to leave in ten minutes, but it may be a little later."

What did that mean? Deanna and I, both veterans of the airline industry, looked at each other. Was there a reason for a possible delay? Was the plane late getting to the airport? Were there mechanical problems? The agent offered no further information.

We found a bench in the waiting area and took a seat. From the window we could see a small plane. It looked like a typical American Airlines Saab 340, only this plane belonged to Aero Mexico.

"That's not so small," Deanna observed.

I agreed. "Doesn't look bad at all. Have you ever taken a shuttle flight?"

"No. I've always heard how small the planes are, but this one doesn't look that bad."

"Smaller than the plane we flew here on but around the same size as a usual American shuttle plane."

Deanna nodded.

Ten minutes went by. No boarding announcement. The waiting area was hot with no air-conditioning. Being spoiled Americans, we were miserable. We watched the gate agent for any sign of boarding. After thirty minutes, we approached him. He assured us the flight would be departing soon. No need for concern.

We returned to our seats. Our pantyhose clung to our legs. Our hair frizzed from the hot muggy air. Sweat dripped down our backs. We continued to wait.

Deanna pulled a scrunchy from her purse and pulled her long, blond hair into a ponytail to get it off her neck. I soon followed suit. We both considered removing our pantyhose wondering if Aero Mexico adhered to the same dress code. I only pondered the idea long enough to remember how white my legs were.

A miserable hour-and-a-half later, the gate agent called to us. It was time to board. We quickly headed for the door and toward the small plane in front of us. We were nearly there when the gate agent hollered at us. In his broken English he informed us it wasn't our plane. Using hand signals, he motioned for us to go around. "The other plane, behind," he kept repeating. "Behind, behind."

Again, we looked at each other and frowned. The plane in front of us was small. How could there be another plane without our seeing it? Still, we followed his flailing arms to the other side of the plane. Lo and behold, there was a tiny, baby plane.

This plane was the smallest either of us had ever seen. My first thought was to look for training wheels. It was about the size of a shuttle bus but not as wide. There was no jetway or even stairs to climb. We were to step up from the ground into the plane, like climbing into a big truck. There was no center aisle. Just eight bench seats in a row. Every two seats had a door. We watched as other passengers, mostly men, stepped up to their seats. Two people to every bench seat, shoulder to shoulder.

When it was our turn, Deanna gracefully climbed into the plane, pulling her flowing skirt in around her long legs. Scooting over, she waited for me. I lifted my leg but quickly found the straight skirt on my shirt-waist dress wasn't going to allow it. I could only lift my leg about six inches before my dress was stretched to capacity. Not enough to reach the plane.

I looked at the ground crew person who was *helping* people climb in. “Do you have a step I could use?”

He looked at me and shrugged, acting like he didn't speak English. I then mimed climbing on a stair and up into the plane. He shook his head. He continued to watch as I made attempts to lift my leg to the floor of the plane. Deanna laughed from her seat above me. No help there. Behind me, two men waited for their turn to board. I was holding up the line, although they watched, enthralled at my situation.

I tried to lift my leg again. It wasn't going to happen.

I looked at the crew member. He continued not to understand.

I looked at Deanna. She had tears in her eyes from laughing.

"Fine," I said. "I'm on vacation. Hope I don't embarrass you." With that proclamation, I hiked my dress high on my thighs, barely covering my bottom, and hoisted myself into the plane.

Deanna let out a howl of laughter. The two men behind me boarded, sitting in the last seat on the plane directly behind me. Their laughter let me know they were also amused.

We pulled the single seatbelt over the two of us and snapped it into place. The ground crew guy shut the door, and the engine started. As we sat hip-to-hip on the bench seat, the walls of the plane hugged our shoulders.

Once in the air, one of the men in the seat behind me, leaned forward. "I think we should be on a first-name status now."

The "checked" luggage was piled in a small area behind the last seat, kind of like the hatchback in a small car. Several passengers called back to ask the men behind me to verify their bags were on board. One passenger called back, "Is there a black bag with a brown leather strap?"

The men behind me turned around and looked. "Yes, I see a black bag with a brown leather strap."

Another passenger called, "Do you see a navy-blue bag with a red scarf tied to the handle?"

"Yes, navy with red scarf is here."

And so, it went until every bag had been accounted for. Remember, we had a total of sixteen passengers, lined up in rows of bench seats that just fit between the wall of the plane and the doors. This whole exercise took less than five minutes.

Shortly after take-off, Deanna noticed air blowing on us. "At least we have air-conditioning."

I looked above me for the source of the air, hoping to adjust it to blow directly on me. I couldn't find the air adjustment thingy. I looked above the heads of the people in front of me. Nope, none above their heads either. With a knot in my stomach, I began looking for the source of the blowing air. I moved my hand around the edge of the door beside me. Air was blowing in from outside. The door wasn't sealed. I elbowed Deanna to inform her of my find. She started laughing again. This time it was a nervous laugh.

I joined her. We had to laugh to keep from freaking out! By this time, we were giddy. We laughed at everything.

The plane flew low over the ocean. The water was so clear you could see the bottom of the Caribbean below us. We watched as white-tipped waves rolled to the beach. As we flew over land, we could see people. Not as tiny dots but as people.

"I think I can read the license plates on the cars," I exclaimed.

The men behind us joked with us. They were from Canada. We exchanged names and found out we were staying at the same hotel.

Finally, we landed. It was easier to get out of the plane. Removing my fashionable high-heeled shoes, I jumped. We grabbed our bags from the plane's hatchback and found a cab.

Hot and sweaty we dragged ourselves through the hotel lobby, we noticed our friends at the bar. Obviously, they hadn't missed us too much. We found our room and changed into fresh clothes. Shorts and tank tops—appropriate for vacationing on an island. Then we joined our friends.

Our trip was wonderful. The water was warm, the sun baked down on us, and the nightlife was fun. We ran into our Canadian friends several times over the next few days.

We were all sad for our adventure to end. I especially hated having to pull pantyhose over my sunburned legs for the flight home.

The five of us returned to Cozumel many times after that

first trip. We found an inexpensive Aero Mexico flight from Dallas to Cozumel that became our go-to. Jacqueline quit her job and moved to the island to teach English to the Mexican children. I never saw another plane as tiny as our little shuttle on that trip. I also never again flew wearing a tight skirt.

In Pursuit of Toilet Paper

by Debbie Anderson

For many years, toilet paper has been taken for granted. At least in the United States. It is considered a necessity, a must-have. However, it is not discussed or mentioned unless someone runs out.

The familiar call from the bathroom, “Honey, I’m out of toilet paper,” is commonly heard in most homes from time to time. Or a child’s panicked voice coming from behind the closed door, “Mom, there’s no toilet paper,” has caused many a mother to jump up from what she’s doing to save the poor child from sitting in distress. These are not examples of a toilet-paper shortage, just normal everyday occurrences in modern times.

There have been toilet-paper shortages in the past. In 1973, Johnny Carson joked about a lack of toilet paper during his monologue after comments made by Wisconsin congressman Harold V. Froehlich about the possibility.

Subsequently, consumers purchased abnormal amounts, causing an actual shortage in the United States for several months.

(Wikipedia, https://en.wikipedia.org/wiki/Toilet_paper.)

Personally, I don't remember any talk of a toilet paper shortage. I was seventeen in 1973, old enough to notice these things. I remember the fuel crisis—having to get gas (the type one puts in their car) on odd or even days, depending on your address. I do not remember a scarcity of toilet paper. Obviously, the shortfall didn't affect my house.

This year, the Corona Virus has caused a real shortage of toilet paper. The issue is discussed on the news, in homes, and on many phone calls. Everyone knows about this shocking loss of flushable tissue.

Suddenly, we find empty shelves where toilet paper once rested. Public restrooms are being raided for the rough, commercial-grade rolls. This may be part of the reason we have been ordered to stay home. I'm sure the cost of stolen toilet paper is causing many businesses to shut their doors.

Recently, I did find a few rolls at Walmart. They were so small, I'm not sure they would last a day at my house where I'm the only user. I don't want to think about the homes with families trying to make do with these tiny packages.

Fortunately, I had bought a sixteen-roll package of mega-sized toilet paper, before the Pandemic. I'm the only one living in my house, but I still always buy the large packages of mega rolls. It's not that I'm afraid of a shortage. I just don't like to buy toilet paper. So, when I first heard about a scarcity, I didn't pay much attention. I was sitting comfortably, happily using my super-strong, yet soft and absorbent paper.

Last week, I realized I was down to my last four rolls. As I changed the cardboard roll to a full one, I considered it might be time to buy more toilet paper. No problem.

I live in a small town in rural America. People here are levelheaded. No one is going to hoard this precious commodity. That type of hysteria is for the big cities where people are prone to crowd mentality.

I made my list of other items I needed, donned my face mask, and headed for the store. First, I stopped at my local grocery store. I picked up meat, bread, and almond milk before heading for the toilet paper aisle. Gasp! The toilet paper was gone! The whole paper aisle was empty. I stood glaring at the empty shelves, amazed at how big they were. Not only was the all-important paper gone, but so were the paper towels, napkins, and wet wipes. I walked down the aisle, hoping to find a paper item wedged into a crack or on the back of a top shelf but to no avail.

I took a deep breath and headed for the drug store. I needed to pick up a prescription anyway. I don't normally buy toilet paper at the drug store, but occasionally they have a great sale, and I add it to my cart.

I quickly made my way to the paper aisle, I saw two women, fighting over a four-pack. Pushing and pulling and screaming names I will have to look up in my dictionary, the women managed to break the package open causing the four rolls to fall to the floor.

A third women jumped onto one roll, giving the others a threatening glare with glazed eyes. "Mine!" she growled. I watched as she shoved the two-ply roll into her large purse and backed out of the aisle. The original two ladies looked at each other and grabbed the other rolls from the floor, watching each other as they, too, backed out of the aisle with their treasure.

I took a minute to process what I had witnessed. Regaining my wits, I walked down the empty row. Again, paper of all kinds was gone. I considered briefly checking the stationary row but pushed that thought away, purchased my prescription, and left the store.

Buckling my seat belt, I took another cleansing breath.

Breathe in slowly—hold it —then out through the mouth—slowly. Now on a mission, I headed for Walmart. I am not a Walmart fan. I hate the crowds. I hate standing in line to check out. I hate all the items strategically placed to cause customers to buy more. This was a last resort. Well, maybe not a last resort. There were other stores in town, but it was the one place to logically have toilet paper.

I stood in line while an associate counted people entering the store. I must have been within the current limit because I was given the go-ahead. I was sure the store would be nearly empty of customers because of this process of counting. I was wrong. It was nearly as crowded as it normally is on a weekday morning. I rushed to the back of the store to get computer ink, then straight to the paper aisle.

At first, I thought the aisle was empty. The sections that usually stocked, Charmin, Northern, and Scott's, were empty. Even the Great Value was gone. My shoulders sagged. Ready to accept my defeat I saw a few small packages at the end of the aisle. I looked around to see if anyone else had noticed.

Nonchalantly, I moved toward the four-roll packages. Grabbing one of the packs, I realized this was a trick. The small package held four pathetic-looking rolls. The cardboard centers were nice and big, but the paper was noticeably lacking. The package wouldn't last a week. I considered buying several packages. They were priced at 68 cents. (They weren't worth that much.) Then I saw the "Attention Customers" notice taped to the shelf. No more than one package per shopper. I sat the package back on the shelf.

By this time, I was ready to go home. I was a failure in the search for TP. As I drove, I tried to think of alternatives. I remembered the outhouse at my great grandmother's. It was stocked with *Sears-Roebuck* catalogs. Not only for wiping purposes but reading. Today Sears-Roebuck is a thing of the past. Plus, most modern septic tanks would clog if we flushed catalog pages.

My mind went to the colored toilet paper of the sixties and seventies. *Whatever happened to those pretty pastel rolls that matched our bathroom décor?*

Back in the day, bathrooms were color-coordinated. If you had blue walls, you also had blue towels, blue counter tops, blue shower curtains and most importantly—blue toilet paper.

It was rare to find a white roll. It would stand out. A white spot in an otherwise colored room. In the early eighties a doctor suggested the dyes in the paper could be harmful to the skin. Environmental reasons were also cited. Slowly, white replaced the pretty colors.

Scott sold colored toilet paper until 2006. Pink toilet paper is still popular in France. And a brand called *Renovo* recently began producing toilet paper in bright, bold colors as well as black and brown. The price is high, $16.20 per six-pack. But in this time of need, the price may not be a consideration.
(https://www.apartmenttherapy.com/colored-toilet-paper-history-255476)

I wonder whatever happened to all that colored paper that *wasn't* sold in the eighties. Is it all stored in a warehouse some place, waiting for the right time to bring it out and save the day? Or was it all sent to Africa or some third-world country that didn't have toilet paper?

I pulled into a Dollar General on my way home. I always stopped there to buy Hostess Sno Balls. Today was no exception. I needed a Sno Ball after all I had been through. I pushed through the door and walked the aisles in case there was something I needed.

As I hit the paper aisle, I stopped and stared. There in front of me was the elusive toilet paper. Not the mostly-cardboard-roll type but real mega-sized rolls. There was a sign taped to the shelves advising customers to limit their purchase to two packages. I picked up one package, a sixteen-pack of mega-sized, strong, white toilet paper. I'm sure I heard angels singing! It was real, and it was mine!

I could have purchased two packages, but I didn't. I chose instead to leave the rest for others who were also in need. One sixteen-count, mega package would last me at least a month. No need to be greedy.

I left the store singing. As I drove home, munching on my Sno Ball, I still wonder about the colored toilet paper. It might be nice to color coordinate the bathroom. But for now, I'll be satisfied with just plain white.

Snake Eyes

by Debbie Anderson

The sun beat down from the August sky. Temperatures hovered around one hundred to one hundred five degrees. The dry, heated air made it impossible to breathe. My parents came to visit me in this oven known as Oklahoma.

I was scheduled for surgery, so my parents made the long trip from Illinois to take care of me. They planned to stay four to six weeks or as long as it took for me to get back on my feet.

The surgery went well. I went home without pain and very little discomfort. My parents stayed to make sure I really was okay, assuming I was still under the influence of the pain medicine from the procedure. I think they were a little disappointed. I felt fine. But they wanted to take care of me.

I was not allowed to carry laundry to the washing machine, sweep floors, or run the vacuum cleaner. Mom and Dad kept telling me to rest. "Don't you need a nap?" Mom would ask. Then she would fall asleep on the couch beside me.

After a few days, Dad wanted to mow my yard and trim some trees. My rotting, backyard deck needed to be torn down. Dad was in his element. This was what he enjoyed doing. I warned him not to mow or do yard work during the extreme heat. He assured me he would get up early before it was too hot. Obviously, he's not from Oklahoma. He did get up bright and early only to find temperatures already in the nineties.

He grew up on a farm in Nebraska. Summers could be grueling. Cutting hay and lifting hay bales are hard work, especially in the extreme heat. There is a reason farmers have *farmer's tans*. It may have been many years since his days on the farm, but he wasn't afraid of a little heat. Out he went to mow the lawn.

I have a large yard in the country. Normally, it takes around two hours to mow using my riding lawn mower. But the grass was tall. It was going to have to be mowed more than once to get it back under control. Mom and I worried as we watched him from the window in the air-conditioned living room. After an hour, Mom took him a large glass of ice water and asked if he was ready to come in.

"Not yet. I've still got the back yard to do." He handed her back the glass and jumped back on the mower.

After another hour, Mom convinced him he needed to take a break and cool off.

Dad agreed and came in. We watched some Westerns on television and had some lunch. He loaded the dishwasher while Mom swept the floors and cleaned the bathroom. I sat in my chair *resting.* I was not allowed to do anything.

The second day, Dad was up early, eager to start on my deck. He took his tools to the backyard and began tearing it down. He probably wouldn't have needed his tools. It was coming apart in his hands, but eventually he would get to the frame and it would take a little more than elbow grease.

Mom and I watched from the dining room window as he worked. It was another steamer of a day. Dad worried us working in the heat.

At one point, Dad lifted a part of a tree trunk that sat in front of the deck. I put planters on the tree pieces, but now they were going to be moved along with the deck. He lifted the stump and quickly dropped it back where it was. He ran to his toolbox. Not finding what he needed, he ran to his car, retrieving his tire iron. Stopping at the back door, he called, "Do you have a hoe or a shovel?"

"Not anymore," I answered. "Do you want me to go buy one?"

He shook his head and ran back to the stump. This time the tire iron was high in the air when he moved the wood. Down came the tire iron onto the head of a large water moccasin. He bashed the snake several times to make sure it was dead. Then taking a breath, he came inside to inform us of his find.

Immediately, Mom and I ran out to see the snake. I grabbed my camera. "Can you hold it up so we can see how big it is?"

"Are you sure it's dead?" Mom asked.

Dad carefully took the snake by the tail and held it up until it was fully extended. His arm was higher than his head. The snake must have been over six-foot long. Then he threw it into the burn pile to be cremated.

Mom and I spent our time, sending pictures to the rest of my siblings and grandkids. Dad finished tearing down the deck and added the rotted wood to the pile to be burned.

Later that afternoon, he started to gather the bricks that had lined my flower garden in the front yard. The flowers were gone, and the bricks were falling into the grass. Mom went to help him.

All at once, Mom flew into the house looking for her phone. Dad found another snake! Grabbing my phone, I ran out to see how big this one was. It ended up being about a foot long. Just a baby compared to the daddy snake in the back yard. Dad said he had been raking up the dead grass and leaves by the edge of the house. He saw what he thought was a worm and tried to pull it out. Every time he raked over it; the *worm* tried to strike the rake. He realized worms don't strike; snakes do. Again, he bashed the little snake in the head and pulled it out of the hole. What first looked like a six-inch worm, was a twelve-inch water moccasin.

"You better watch for snakes," he instructed. "There are probably many more where those two came from."

"Don't worry!" I assured him. "I hate snakes!"

"So do I!" he said.

Before long, my parents realized I really was fine. And although they would like to have stayed and taken care of me longer, it wasn't necessary. Dad had his own lawn to mow, and they wanted to travel and see my other siblings.

I was sorry to see them go.

***

The next day I started into my laundry room to get something from my freezer. As I took my first step, I saw it—a large green snake stretched out in front of the dryer. I froze. I stared at it. It stared back at me. Its forked tongue flicked, but it didn't move. I was afraid to take my eyes away. I didn't want him to crawl under the washer or dryer or freezer. I knew if I didn't get rid of him, he could get away, and I'd have to watch out for him in every room in the house.

Our eyes were locked on each other. Quickly I considered my options. I could run (my first choice, but it really didn't solve the problem). I could grab the broom and try to sweep him out the back door (another temporary fix.) Or I could bash its head in, assuring he would not be coming back.

Okay, it's obvious which solution would be most effective. I still didn't have a hoe or a shovel. What did I have that would work to bash it? I mentally inventoried my tool chest. I did have a hammer. That would be hard enough. It was in the garage, right next door to the laundry room. But what if the snake got away while I was gone?

Our eyes had not left each other since I discovered the snake. I tried to tell myself that I had probably hypnotized him. I pointed my finger at him and said, "Don't you move! You stay right where you are until I get back." The snake flicked his tongue at me, but he didn't move.

I darted out the door into the garage, grabbed my hammer, and ran back. The snake had not moved. He continued to stare at me.

Then I realized, if I got close enough to bash him with a hammer, I'd also be close enough for him to strike me. *Now what?*

I looked around the room and saw my broom and long-handled dustpan. That was it. The long handle would allow me to hold the snake with the dustpan. If I trapped him behind his head, I could hold him with one hand and bash him with the hammer in the other.

I took a deep breath. My heart was about to burst from my chest. I continued staring at the snake, talking to him with a reassuring voice. Taking one small step at a time, I moved as close to the creature as possible. When I knew I didn't dare go any closer, I lowered the dustpan slowly down behind his head. It took all my weight to keep the flimsy plastic dustpan in place. The snake wasn't happy. He writhed beneath the plastic, showing his fangs and letting me know he wasn't pleased.

I knew I couldn't let up even a little bit because he would get loose, and I would be the subject of his wrath. I mustered up all my courage. I brought the hammer down on his head. One strike, two, three … the snake shook his tail and exposed his fangs. I was amazed at his strength and endurance. I continued to bash him with the hammer until he quit moving. Carefully, I lifted the dustpan, expecting the snake to suddenly start moving again. But he was still. I shivered.

I took pictures of my kill. Retrieving tongs from the kitchen, I picked him up, went out the back door, and threw him over the fence. It took hours for the adrenaline to subside.

The following day, I did laundry. I took a load from the dryer and set it on the table to be folded. Then I went back to put the load in the washer into dryer. As I stepped into the room, I noticed something in the corner of my eye. There between the dryer and the wall was the face of another snake!

Fortunately, I bought a hoe earlier in the day for just such an occasion. It was sitting in the laundry room so I wouldn't have to retrieve it from the garage. Grabbing the handle, I carefully moved toward the dryer. The snake started to back up.

"Oh no you don't!" I hollered.

I brought the hoe down on the snake and pulled it out from beside the dryer. He wasn't going to go without a fight. I leaned on the hoe. I wanted to chop off his head. He shook his tail from side to side. Showing his fangs, he looked at me with his beady black eyes. His tongue flicked in and out. I was afraid he was going to get away. The hoe wasn't sharp enough to do much chopping, so again I leaned into the handle in an effort to crush him. It was a battle to the death. My arms ached by the time his head was crushed. He was bigger than the one from the night before.

Again, I took a picture. I grabbed the tongs to take him outside, but it was raining. I decided I wasn't going out in the rain, and instead, I tried to throw him toward the fence where I could find him the next morning. I cleaned the blood off the floor and went to bed forgetting all about the load of clothes I wanted to dry.

First thing the next morning, I called the exterminator. He informed me there wasn't much that he could do to get rid of snakes, but he would try. I showed him where the snakes had been. I told him I thought they were coming in somewhere by the dryer. He didn't agree but humored me.

Pulling out the dryer he looked behind it. "I think you're right. They are coming in through your dryer vent."

He opened the back door to take a look from outside. There in front of him was the snake from the night before. He jumped back in the house pushing me behind him. "Is that the snake you killed last night?"

"That's him."

"That's a copperhead!" he stepped outside, gingerly picking up the dead snake by its tail and throwing it over the fence. "Was the other one like this one?"

"Yes, not quite as big but close."

He nodded. "Have you seen many mice?"

"More than usual. They come from the field next door."

"That's the problem. The snakes are following the mice. They come in through your dryer vent, and the snakes come in too."

"But how is that possible? If they're coming in through the vent, wouldn't they get caught in the dryer hose?"

He didn't answer me.

"I'm going to put out some mouse killer. Once the mice are gone, you won't have any more problems with snakes." He went about distributing mouse killer throughout the house, leaving me a bag of extra packets if I saw any more mice.

"What about snake repellent?"

"I don't believe in it. I haven't noticed it works very well. If you want to try it, go pick some up at Home Depot. It's not going to hurt anything."

As soon as he left, I went to Home Depot. I asked one of the associates for snake repellent. He wasn't sure where it was. Another customer heard me ask and told me to buy mothballs.

“Mothballs are much cheaper,” she said, “and snakes don’t like it. Just put it around the exterior of your house and by your garage door. The snakes will stay away.

They do melt when they get wet, so you’ll have to put fresh mothballs out after it rains.”

I thanked her and bought an industrial size container of mothballs. I haven’t had any more snakes in the house. I replaced the hose from the dryer. Mice had eaten through the hose leaving a hole about three inches in diameter, more than big enough for snakes. I sprinkled mothballs around the circumference of the house, and it seems to have worked. I haven’t had any mice or snakes since.

I sent pictures of the snakes to my parents and family. Dad told me I was much braver than he was. I know that’s not true, but it was nice of him to say so.

There are still snakes in the field around my house. This year one neighbor told me he killed nine copperheads in his garage. Another neighbor said he killed a water moccasin while he was mowing his lawn. A friend told me he got up in the middle of the night and found a snake in his toilet! Maybe I’ll have to keep a hoe in the bathroom, too.

Yogi and Boo Boo

by Debbie Anderson

What a great night for shopping! Margo thought on her way to her favorite store. After months of everything being shut down, the governor decided to slowly open her state. Citizens were advised to continue to practice social distancing and wear masks to keep the horrible COVID-19 from infecting more victims.

Margo saw that Target was again open for business. She hated wearing her face mask, but she would comply if it meant shopping again. Tonight was a perfect summer night, warm with a light breeze. The rain of the last three days was gone, leaving a clean, fresh scent in the air.

The traffic light ahead of her turned red, and Margo pulled to a stop. She glanced in the rearview mirror to check her hair. A few tosses with her fingers, and she was satisfied with her appearance. Then she saw them, two, uh, *beings* were in the car behind her.

Photo by Miriam Esparcio, unsplash.com

Beings was the best word to describe them. They didn't really look like people or animals. The only thing she could compare them with would be alien beings from another world. At least the pictures she saw in books and movies. She hadn't actually believed in them, but what were those things? The car interior glowed allowing Margo to see the beings well. Then she realized it wasn't the car interior that glowed. It was them!

The light turned green, and Margo hit the gas. The other car stayed behind her as if somehow attached to her bumper. Target was still a few miles away. Margo hoped to lose these losers before she got there.

She noticed she was passing a Walmart. At the last possible moment, she turned the wheel, nearly doing a donut in the middle of the traffic but straightening her car in time to enter Walmart's parking lot. Pulling into a parking space, she continued to look over her shoulder for the beings.

"I think I lost them." Margo gave a sigh of relief. She grabbed her purse and started to open the door, but it wouldn't budge. She was about to give it a shove with her shoulder when she noticed the occupants of the car in front of her. It was them!

Frantically, she banged against the door. When that didn't work, she tried to start the car, but it wouldn't turn on. She pounded on the steering wheel in frustration.

"That must hurt," said a voice behind her.

"This must be the violence we were warned about," said another voice. They broke into giggles.

Margo looked at the car in front of her. It was empty. Lifting her gaze to the mirror she saw the glowing—*things*—were now in her back seat.

"AAAIIIIEEEHHH!" Margo screamed.

"AAAIIIIEEEHHH!" screamed the creatures.

"She scared me," said one.

"Don't be scared. Act like a statue."

"What's a statue?"

"Remember the pictures of the men on horses that

wouldn't move? That's a statue. If we act like one, maybe she won't turn us into one."

Margo stared at the glowing things in her back seat. "What are you?" She asked trembling. "What do you want from me?"

The glowing statues in the back seat looked at each other.

The small one whispered, "She's talking to us, Yogi."

The bigger one put his finger to where his mouth should be and stayed perfectly still.

"Oh, I get it. We're going to pretend we're statues some more." The small one froze into position in the back seat.

Margo turned around to stare at them.

"I know you're not statues."

The two things looked at each other, then quickly went back to statue pose.

"Please don't take me to your ship," cried Margo. "I get motion sickness."

"What's motion sickness?" asked the big one.

"Shhh!" said the little one, "She'll hear you."

"Stop playing that silly game and talk to me! What do you want?"

"I thought earthlings liked to play games, like Statues, Jacks, Mother May I, Red Rover …" the big one said.

"Well, I don't!" Margo yelled. "So, stop it!"

The things returned to being statues.

"London Bridge, Ring Around the Rosey…" continued the big one in a whisper.

"Stop it!"

"These earthlings are violent!" said the small one.

"I'm not violent!" Margo yelled. "I don't believe in violence! Now tell me who you are and what you want." Margo wasn't afraid anymore. These creatures were not very threatening.

"I don't think I like your tone," said the big one, crossing his arms over his chest.

"Uh, she doesn't look so bad," the little one replied. "We came to make contact with real humanoids, and now we have. Let's get to know her better."

The big one looked down at the small one. "You think it's safe?"

"Look at her! What could she possibly do to us?"

Margo rolled her eyes. "Okay, let's start from the beginning. My name's Margo. I live here. Who are you?"

The little one scooted forward on the seat. "That's Yogi, and I'm Boo Boo. We don't live here, at least not yet."

"Wait. Yogi and Boo Boo, from the cartoons?"

"That's right, Mr. Ranger, Sir!"

"I'm not Mr. Ranger. I'm Margo, remember? Why are you using cartoon names? Don't you have real names?"

"Of course, we do. But we wanted to fit in, so we chose humanoid names."

"Those are cartoon names. Don't you know the difference between cartoons and real people?"

Yogi and Boo Boo glanced at each other. "Are you trying to trick us?" asked Yogi.

"No. Cartoons aren't real. Humans are."

"Now I know you're trying to trick us. We've been watching cartoons for years. They are real. We've seen them.

"Where did you see them? Look around you, do you see any cartoons walking around?"

"She's right, Yogi! I don't see any cartoons anywhere."

Yogi brought his hand-looking appendage to where his chin might be. It sank right into his face. Pulling it out again, he addressed Boo Boo, "Maybe they don't like cartoons around here. Maybe all the cartoons live in Jellystone Park."

Margo rolled her eyes. "We don't keep cartoons in Jellystone Park. Cartoons aren't real. They're pretend."

"What is pre-tend?" asked Yogi, trying the word on his tongue.

"Cartoons," replied Margo. "Trust me, I live here. I would know."

Yogi squinted his large eyes, not sure what to believe.

"So why are you here?" asked Margo.

"We want to hang out with you and see if we can fit in," answered Boo Boo.

"We've been studying earth for thousands of years. Now it's time to visit."

"Yeah, most of our vacation spots back home are about gone. You know, thanks to pollution and global warming. Recently we noticed our planet was starting to sputter. I think it's just worn out. So here we are."

Margo looked from Yogi to Boo Boo in disbelief. "You've got global warming, too?"

"Oh yes! For thousands of years now. Like I said, our planet is about dead." Yogi looked down. Margo could sense his sadness.

"Why would you think this planet will be any better?" Margo asked.

"We don't. We just know it's not as bad as our planet. It'll buy us some time to find another place." Boo Boo touched his glowing hand to Margo's cheek. "Soft," he said. "You must use Ivory Soap. The soap that floats."

Margo jerked back. "Commercials, too? By the way, that

Ivory Soap thing is really old. No one cares if it floats any more. Don't you watch anything new?"

"Do you know how long it takes to get a signal from earth to a satellite and on to us? A long time!" Boo Boo stated, his feelings hurt.

Margo felt bad for making fun of her visitors. "Okay, listen. You want to hang out? You might as well come into Walmart with me."

Yogi and Boo Boo looked up excitedly. "Really? We can come with you?"

"Yes, but there are a few things you need to know. We're having a COVID-19 outbreak, so we have to wear face masks to go inside."

"You mean like the Lone Ranger?" asked Yogi.

"Kind of. But instead of wearing the mask over your eyes you need to wear them over your mouth." Margo quickly put her mask on to demonstrate.

She handed her new friends each a mask. She knew they didn't have mouths, but she hadn't thought of them not having ears. She took the masks away and handed them each a bandana. "We'll just tie these behind your heads."

"Like the bad guys on the Rifleman," Yogi bounced up and down with glee. "Do we get guns too?"

"No guns!"

"Are we going to rob the place? Get the loot?"

"Hands in the air!" added Boo Boo.

"We're not robbing anything!" Margo took a deep breath. "We are going shopping. We will pay for our purchases before we leave. Now quit kidding around!"

Yogi and Boo Boo hung their heads.

"Okay, you stay with me. We need to keep six feet between us and the shoppers in front of us. We don't want to catch a virus."

"Six feet?" asked Yogi. "How do we do that? You have two feet. We don't have any feet. That means we're going to have to find more feet."

"No, I'm talking about the measurement of six feet. Not the feet at the end of our legs. What do you mean you don't have any feet?"

"Do you mean the measurement or the things at the end of our legs?" asked Boo Boo.

"The things at the end of our legs," replied Margo.

"Oh, those. We don't have any."

"Then how do you get around?"

Yogi and Boo Boo looked at each other and shrugged. "We just do!" Boo Boo answered with a frown.

Margo looked over the seat. Sure enough, no feet.

"Alright, let's go. Follow my lead. Don't stray off by

yourselves. Got it?”

“Got what?” asked Yogi.

Margo’s door opened easily making her believe her two new acquaintances caused the problem she had earlier. As she climbed out of the car, Yogi and Boo Boo hovered beside her.

“Follow me.”

Margo headed for the store, Yogi and Boo Boo floating beside her. “This should be interesting.”

Yogi and Boo Boo watched in awe as the door opened on its own. “Just like back home,” Boo Boo whispered.

Margo spent the next hour looking for her guests or taking objects away from them. The toy department was the worst.

Before she could stop them, they each had a slinky out of the box and were juggling it from one hand to the other. “It’s slinky, it’s slinky, for fun it's a wonderful toy ...” sang Boo Boo.

“Hey, Boo Boo, look at this,” called Yogi. Then he juggled the slinky from his hand into his mouth. The toy disappeared.

“Hey, you can’t do that!” called a young kid with a Walmart badge that read *Roger.*

“Why not?” asked Yogi.

The kid looked puzzled for a second. “I don’t know. You just can’t. Now give me that slinky!”

“Give him the slinky!” shouted Margo. “You need to listen to me.”

“Fine,” Yogi pouted. He took a deep breath and blew out the slinky with such force it knocked the kid into the Hot Wheel stand. The slinky whipped around the kid securing him to the display.

“Let’s go. Both of you. March!” Margo ordered, pointing to the front of the store.

Hanging their heads, Yogi and Boo Boo followed Margo. She stopped at the check-out long enough to tell the clerk she changed her mind and leave her shopping cart. She stomped to the car, the troublemakers hovering behind her.

“Now where are we going?” asked Yogi.

“*I’m* going home. I don’t know where *you* are going.” Margo huffed.

As they returned to Margo’s car, she pointed to the car parked in front of her. “That’s *yours*. It’s been interesting knowing you. Now, go.”

She climbed into her car and started the engine. So much for shopping. Turning to look over her shoulder and back out of her parking space, she found Yogi and Boo Boo in the back seat.

Margo stomped on her brake. “What are you doing here? I told you to get in *your* car. Leave me alone!”

“We’re sorry!” Boo Boo said sheepishly. “We didn’t mean to cause any trouble.”

“This is the most fun we’ve had in thousands of years. We weren’t trying to make you mad,” added Yogi.

Margo closed her eyes and counted to ten. She took a deep breath. “I know you didn’t mean it, but that’s just not how we act on earth.”

The car was quiet for a moment while everyone thought about the shopping trip.

“That one kid, the one with the shirt that showed his belly?”

“Yeah. What about him?”

“He stuck a marble in his nose,” finished Yogi.

“Did you see the man with his pants hanging down below his underwear? That was weird. Is that how people dress? I never saw Mr. Ranger wear his pants like that,” said Boo Boo.

“Or the Rifleman or the Lone Ranger,” added Yogi.

“I never understood what that fashion statement was all about,” added Margo.

“What about the two girls in their underwear?” Boo Boo went on. Their masks covered more than their underwear.

Seemed strange."

"Those were bathing suits, not underwear, but you're right, their masks were bigger, and no, that is not acceptable attire for shopping."

"It was kind of neat being able to help yourself to snacks," said Yogi.

Margo and Boo Boo both looked up. "What snacks?" They asked in unison.

"In the area with all those tanks of water with things swimming in them.

"The pet department?" Margo asked in horror. "There were no snacks there—only fish and hamsters. People buy them as pets, not to eat!"

"What about that kid with the torn pants? He pulled his mask off, caught one of the little wiggly things..."

"A fish!" said Margo.

"... and put it in his mouth. His friends were laughing. Then they all ate some, too. I thought it must be a free snack."

"Gross! Please tell me you didn't eat one."

"Not exactly," Yogi looked down at his stomach area. "See." He brightened the glow that emanated from his being. As the light increased, Margo watched as a little fish appeared, swimming around inside Yogi. "I was going to save it for later."

Yogi and Boo Boo started to laugh, their glowing heads bouncing up and down. Margo watched. They were having fun. *I could use some fun*.

"Okay guys. Where should we go next? Have you ever had pizza?" And off they went on another great adventure.

ABOUT CLAY CARLEY III

Clay B. Carley III has a Masters in Computer Science and has wanted to be an author of other genres besides computer programs. He retired in 2016 from East Central University after teaching Computer Science for 16 year. His spare time is devoted to reading, writing and raising quail.

To improve his writing, Clay regularly attends the Ada Writers Group and Writing for Fun.

Published humorous short stories include:

Carley, Clay B. "What About Bob?" *Creations*, Ada Writers, 2017.

Carley, Clay B. "The Pitbull, Spot." *Creations*, Ada Writers, 2017.

Carley, Clay B. "Fin or Flipper?" *Creations*, Ada Writers, 2018.

Carley, Clay B. "It Wasn't the Moon." *Creations*, Ada Writers, 2018.

Carley, Clay B. "The One that Got Away, Thank God!" *Creations*, Ada Writers, 2018.

Carley, Clay B. "On the Wrong Side of the Fence." *Creations*, Ada Writers, 2019.

Carley, Clay B. "S. H. Lawrence." *Creations*, Ada Writers, 2019.

Currently working on a full-length thriller.

"Some people have a way with words, and other people ... oh, uh, not have way." — Steve Martin

Almost a Conscientious Objector

by Clay B. Carley III

The Vietnam War was raging in 1970. Violence erupted at antiwar demonstrations. The draft was in full swing and draft-dodgers fled to Canada. Patriotism was under fire. It was the year when I graduated from college with a Bachelor's Degree in Mathematics and, at 22 years old, became eligible for the draft.

I had six choices: one, be drafted; two, leave the country; three, join as a conscientious objector; four, enter a military service of my choosing; five, get married; or, six, injure myself and become ineligible for military service. Although I had strong antiwar feelings, I fit the definition of patriot: "a person who loves, supports, and defends his or her country and its interests with devotion" (https://www.dictionary.com/browse/patriot). I really only had three legitimate choices: declare myself a conscientious objector, be drafted, or enter a military service of my choosing.

I decided to preemptively join and enlisted for a "four-plus-two" in the Navy, that is, four years regular enlistment with a two-year extension. There were benefits to enlisting in this way. One was schooling. I attended "A" school for basic electronics and "C" school for a specific weapons system. Two was at the beginning of my two-year extension, I would get a substantial reenlistment bonus.

During C school, I made friends with an E9 Chief (the highest enlisted rating). He said he had a friend in the Navy assignments office in Washington, D.C. and asked me where I would like to go after school. There was no question. I didn't care where, so long as I was able to work on computers.

January 1972, I finished C school. Since all naval schools that I attended were in my native California, I was surprised that I wasn't assigned to a ship in the Pacific Fleet. Instead, I was assigned to a destroyer escort in the Atlantic Fleet, the U.S.S. Trippe, DE1075. The Trippe was stationed out of Newport, Rhode Island, about as far away from Vietnam as one could get.

My first deployment aboard the Trippe was to San Juan, Puerto Rico, where I enjoyed snorkeling during liberty. Between February and December, the ship was in Boston

Naval Shipyard being retrofitted. The crew and I had a lot of free time to explore Boston. Afterwards, the ship returned to Newport for a short time. The captain then received secret orders, which we could only surmise were for the Trippe to go to Vietnam.

Two days out of port, our assumptions were confirmed. We were Vietnam bound. The first part of the trip seemed like a vacation. The passage through the Panama Canal felt more like being on a cruise ship. I had a lot of time on my hands and enjoyed looking at the scenery, watching as the ship moved from lock to lock of the canal. Once in the Pacific, however, it was back to military activities.

The Trippe joined a West Pac (western Pacific) squadron. We participated in target practice to check our weapons systems. This meant work for me since I was a FTM3 (fire control technician, missiles, third class petty officer). I was part of the group that maintained the Interim Surface-to-Surface Missile (ISSM) system. Although I helped maintain the ISSM fire control computer, my primary responsibility was maintaining the continuous-wave illuminator (CWI) radar that was used to direct a missile's flight. My duty station during exercises and general quarters was at the ISSM console in the Weapons Control Center. It was my responsibility to turn on CWI radar and, when called upon, to launch one of the two ISSM Tartar missiles carried by the Trippe.

The ISSM part of the exercises didn't do well. One missile didn't launch, and the other missed its target. The weapons officer was not happy. He blamed the failures on improper maintenance, including not doing the daily system checks. So, he called in the ISSM system technical representatives (tech reps) to inspect our system.

The tech reps had come aboard from time-to-time to install upgrades to the system. They were always friendly to us and told us the reason for their inspection. My buddies and I weren't worried, however, because we had always done the required maintenance of the system.

The tech reps let us read their report before turning it in to the weapons officer. My ship mates and I were vindicated. The missile that failed to launch was due to a broken switch in the launcher. It could not have been detected except when trying an actual launch.

The weapons officer thought the miss occurred because the CWI radar wasn't generating a strong enough signal for the missiles to follow. After the inspection, however, the tech rep and I had a laugh at the officer's expense. The tech rep said the CWI radar was the best-maintained in the fleet. Also, I had it tuned "too well." It was generating a signal far stronger than any other in the fleet, in fact, it was really “too much” and would melt down the radar dish with prolonged use. He knew I hadn’t done anything wrong, as I was just going by the directions given in the manual. But he said that I should detune the radar a bit.

Our next port-of-call was Hawaii. I saw the USS Arizona Memorial as the Trippe passed by it. We had a couple hours of liberty, so I only got to walk around a bit. However, I did get to walk on one of the beaches.

We had a long stretch at sea after leaving Hawaii. Our next stop was Guam. We were only there for a few hours. I did go into the Post Exchange (PX) to see what they had for sale. All the shelves looked like they were swaying until I got my “land legs.”

Then it was a comparatively short jaunt to our last port-of-call before Vietnam—Olongopo City on Subic Bay, the Philippines. The port was memorable for two things: the smell of raw sewage that assaulted us while still out at sea and the jets that frequently took off. When the pilots kicked in the afterburners, the jets’ exhaust was very impressive with reds and blues, day or night.

The ship spent a couple of days in port. We stocked up on 5-inch 54 ammunition for our forward “cannon,” replenished our food stores, and had two tripod mounted machine guns welded amidships on the upper deck. We were told that the machine guns were for our protection from attacking sampans. All of our other weapons weren't designed for close-up fighting. After stocking up, we headed to Vietnam and took up station patrolling part of the coastline.

The beaches had been designated as exclusion zones. Nothing was allowed on a beach unless authorized by U.S. command. As we patrolled the coast, aerial spotters contacted us from time to time with requests for fire support. These requests were for fire power against enemy tanks on the ground or troop assistance in battle. Our 5-inch 54 was the weapon of choice. I always thought it was like a huge machine gun firing a number of rounds per minute. The shells weighed 75 pounds with the separate powder weighing in at 80 pounds. There was no mistaking when the 5-inch 54 fired, even when someone was inside the steel hull of the ship. No matter where I was, I could always tell when it fired. There was the loud boom, and the recoil caused the ship to shudder.

We had a couple of observers, generally on the flying bridge, who kept an eye on the beaches as we cruised. Also, there was an observation station in the 5-inch 54 turret which was manned 24/7 while patrolling the Vietnam coast.

One day, as we were patrolling the coast, the 5-inch 54 fired half a dozen rounds at the beach. One of my crewmates told me that we had killed a woman, her child, and their dog as they were walking on the beach. I was incensed. I was ready to declare myself a conscientious objector—even though I would probably be thrown in the brig. However, I cooled off enough that I could think straight and decided to wait and confirm what really occurred. Don, one of my friends, was the current 5-inch 54 observer, so I waited for him to get off duty and get an eyewitness account.

Photo supplied by author

Don's story was quite different, thank God. He told me that there was a Viet Cong patrol on the beach. The first high-explosive shell missed, and the patrol began running down the beach, the shells landing at their heels. They made the mistake of jumping behind a sand dune for protection. When the last shell landed, there was nothing left of the dune or the patrol.

That day I relearned one thing and learned something about myself. I relearned not to depend on rumors, especially since the Navy is always rife with them. The thing I learned about myself was there are war time incidents that I could not stomach and would quite willingly stop contributing in a combat capacity

ABOUT BETTY J. CROW

Betty J. Crow is a fiction writer and author of two books of short stories, *The Apple Tree* and *Stranger on the Shore.* She has also published several short stories in compilation books, including *Not Your Mother's Book on Being a Parent, Ann's Cooking from Scratch*, and *Creations 2019*. She is currently working on her first novel, to be titled *Blackthorne Cove*.

Betty grew up on a grain farm near Toledo, Illinois. She lived most of her adult life in Texas, with the exception of time spent in Tennessee and North Carolina. She credits her sixth-grade teacher, Mrs. Everhart, for her interest in writing. Betty is an amateur nature photographer and enjoys travelling the backroads looking for birds and other animals. Betty currently resides in Oklahoma with her husband, Don, and best dog, Gus.

Always Carry a Broom to the Outhouse

by Betty Crow

It was the summer of 1955, shortly after my fifth birthday. We were visiting my grandparents who lived west of Toledo, Illinois. The women were busy cooking in the kitchen, and my brother went to check on the livestock with Grandpa. I was alone, left to explore that forbidden room under the stairs. I was feeling my way through the shadowy darkness when the urge struck. I shouldn't have had that second dipper of water from the bucket in the kitchen, for you see, Grandma's house wasn't equipped with indoor plumbing, and Mother Nature had come to call.

I put off the inevitable as long as I could, but it was soon apparent the time had come to take care of business or embarrass myself. I hurried to the kitchen to get my mom. She would go with me to that dreaded building at the far edge of the lawn.

Not only was the outhouse less than fragrant, I worried

that snakes lurked inside that dark hole, ready to bite my…well you know what. However, that wasn't the most terrifying part of a trip to the toilet. Grandma had geese.

There were probably six or seven of the long-necked creatures, but a hundred couldn't have been more menacing. For those of you who are not familiar with geese, they are better than watch dogs for protecting hearth and home. They threaten their victims by hissing, honking, and flapping their wings, ready to peck the eyes out of short people like me. They may not frighten adults who tower over them, but to those of us who are eye level to open beak, they are more frightening than the scariest monster ever to hide under a bed.

In order to safely reach the outhouse, I needed a protector. I tugged on my mom's skirt.

"Yes?" She asked, without looking down.

"I need to go to the bathroom," I stated matter-of-factly.

"Then go," she responded, still working the pie dough with her hands.

Surprised by her abrupt response, I explained, "I can't. The geese will get me."

"Don't be silly," she said with a chuckle.

"Come on," I said more urgently.

"Run fast. Now go on, I'm busy."

Dancing with need, I repeated my urgent plea, "Come on, Mom."

Grandma Burton was the mother of fourteen, and I was way down the line of already existing grandchildren. Grandma had no patience for whiners. Wordlessly, she clamped her hand over my shoulder and guided me toward the door. Much to my dismay, she pushed open the screen door with her foot, while simultaneously thrusting a broom into my hands and shoving me outside. This was a woman talented in the art of multi-tasking.

"Shoo them away with the broom," was all she said before the door slammed shut behind me.

White knuckled, my tiny fingers gripped the broom handle. I looked around but didn't see the geese. Maybe they had followed my brother. I smiled mischievously to myself and started skipping down the dirt path toward relief. Unfortunately, my glee was short-lived. I was about halfway to my destination when I saw the geese running toward me, their beaks open wide, hissing wickedly. I stopped, frozen in my tracks.

As they came closer, my wits returned. I ran as fast as I could toward that weathered building with the rusty handle. *Please let the door be open*, I pleaded silently, but, of course, it wasn't. With the geese hot on my trail, there was no time to open the door. I took a deep breath and somehow found the courage to turn and face my fear. I straightened my shoulders, held my head high, and wildly waved my weapon back and forth. I walked resolutely toward that mean old gander, and although he didn't back off, he came to a halt, apparently shocked into silence by my madness. His hesitance gave me the time I needed to lift the latch and escape inside the outhouse. I was safe, at least from the geese. Now what about that snake?

Back Porch Sittin'

By Betty Crow

Since retirement, Saturday is no longer a day to rush around cleaning, mowing, or shopping for groceries. Mundane chores are completed during the week. Now it is the day I like to stay home and relax. When weather permits, my day begins on the back porch with a steaming cup of coffee.

Gus, our red-heeler, comes along. He checks the perimeter for danger, before making himself comfortable at my feet. As dawn colors the sky, birds come alive. They are practicing their calls and singing the day awake. A cardinal makes a precarious landing on the edge of the feeder, followed by his lady. He hops off and sits on the fence while she eats her fill. A chickadee joins her, followed by a dark-eyed junco. A larger bird, practicing his menacing moves, swoops down and lands nearby. He utters a high-pitched call, and the other birds quickly disappear. It's the dreaded cowbird.

“Get him, Gus.” I whisper.

Gus swiftly advances toward the enemy. He barks. The cowbird flies to safety in the top of a dead tree. Gus barks some more and then struts back to the porch. “Good dog,” I say and give him a pat on the head. He flops down and closes his eyes. He’s asleep.

A hummingbird roars by, circles, and lands on the new red Hummerdome I found at the hardware store last week. He takes a few sips of nectar before a WWII reenactment begins. Mr. Hummer #2 in a Japanese Zero dives down from the clouds. Mr. Hummer #1 climbs into his Hellcat, and the fight is on. They forget they have an audience. After a few passes, they each retire to the fence. One is on the north side, the other on the south. They prepare to fight another war—they’re off for round two.

Gus jumps up, runs toward the west perimeter, and starts barking his mean bark. It’s the neighbor’s bull. I silence the dog before the bull charges through the rickety fence. The bull wanders off.

The sound of hooves beating against hard earth distracts me. The pasture has morphed into the racetrack at Churchill Downs. Two horses are running across the pasture at top speed—side by side—racing. Whiskey pulls ahead. With his muscled body straining, Nero fights back to take the lead. By the time they reach the pond, I decide Whiskey is the winner by a nose. At the track it would have been a photo finish. The thunder of hooves subsides. Nero snorts, kicks, and nips Whiskey on the neck. Whiskey reciprocates with a nip to Nero's nose. With a shake of his head, Whiskey walks over to the pond. Nero follows. In tandem, they bend down to get a drink.

Don, coffee in hand, comes outside. "Any excitement this morning?"

"Actually, yes." I say. "Have a seat, and I'll tell you all about it."

He sits. I talk. We laugh. It's another relaxing day of back porch sittin'.

Cindy Kicker

by Betty J. Crow

Friday was a quiet day at work. The weather was wicked. Those able to stay inside, wouldn't go out. Few were thrilled to come to the courthouse on a good day. Icy roads offered a good excuse to stay home. I was busy working on my inbox when the telephone rang.

"Circuit Clerk's office."

"Mom? Are you busy?"

I could tell from her voice she was excited. "Hi Tami. What's up?"

"I kicked the door in."

"You what?"

"I kicked the door in," she repeated.

"Oh," I said. "What door?"

"The house door."

"The front door?"

"No, the garage door."

"Your garage door?"

"Yes!"

Confused, I asked, "Why?"

"I locked myself out. I dropped the older kids off at school, and when I got home, discovered I forgot to pick up the house key when I left."

In my motherly voice I asked, "Don't you check these things before you leave the house?"

"We were running late, and Luke was having a less-than-cooperative morning. It was too cold for him to be outside while I figured out how to unlock the door. So, I kicked the door in. Aren't you excited? Those Cindy Crawford workout DVDs have strengthened my legs. It only took five kicks before the door came out of the frame."

I envisioned the garage door dangling precariously, ready to fall on one of my precious grandchildren's head. "And that's the only solution you could come up with?"

"I left my phone on the kitchen counter. Besides, Chris is out of town on business until tomorrow."

"Well, why not use the neighbor's telephone to call a locksmith?"

"Oh. Well. I didn't think of that."

"Have you called someone to fix the garage door? It could fall and cause serious injury."

"It can't fall, it's still on the hinges."

"Garage doors don't have hinges, do they?"

"Not THAT garage door. The one that comes into the house."

"Oh," I said.

"Still, you should call someone to fix the door. How will you lock it?"

"I can lock the side entry. No one can get in. Chris will be home at 2:00 A.M. tonight. He will have time to fix it in the morning before I take him to the airport. He's going to the Czech Republic for a week."

"At least you can secure the house."

Obviously annoyed by my failure to acknowledge her ability to kick down a door, she asked, "Don't you think it's exciting? I have the strength to kick in a door? Maybe I missed my calling. Maybe I should have been a policewoman?"

"Cindy Kicker, Policewoman. It does have a nice ring to it."

Chris fixed the door and repacked his suitcase. They had thirty minutes to get to the airport. No problem. Cindy kicked the accelerator to the floor. They arrived with five minutes to spare. Cindy Kicker had saved the day—again.

GaGa Gets a Visit

by Betty Crow

The house was quiet when the van pulled up. Out hop three grandchildren, all race to get simultaneous hugs. I collapse onto the steps, surrounded by arms and legs, smothered in kisses. Another, the youngest, is dropped onto the pile by his mother, who is happy to be free, if only for a few minutes. Now there are four.

The quiet house is full of little voices, proclaiming their love, telling me they missed me, while asking for apple juice.

My neat house gradually becomes cluttered with shoes, toys, clothes, coloring books, crayons, and Thomas the Train movies.

The once spot-free carpet now has a stain from one rather nasty nosebleed, drips of apple and orange juice, and a bit of smashed banana in front of the TV.

The cushions are no longer on the sofa or chairs. In their

place are kids hopping up and down, pretending they are jumping on their trampoline back home.

The room is filled with mom and grandma voicing concerns about broken arms, legs, and necks. Threats of time-outs and no ice cream treats fall on deaf ears.

The coffee table and side tables no longer hold breakables, they are all broken. Now they hold scratches made by race cars, tractors, and helicopters in motion.

Curtains are for hiding behind, window ledges for climbing on. Window blinds are raised and lowered at lightning speed.

The kitchen floor is covered in crumbs, spills, and Aunt Jemima syrup. Dishes are tossed in the sink and stacked on counters. Spilled drinks run down the front of stark white cabinets. There is even a smashed strawberry under the area rug.

The bathroom floor is littered with wet towels. Someone has unrolled half the roll of toilet paper. Tissues have been pulled from their box and left to dissolve in pools of water left by dripping hands.

The ceiling fan in the guest bedroom now jumps and wiggles like a hula dancer. The pull chain made the perfect vine for Tarzan to swing through the jungle.

***

The van is loaded, the house is quiet. I'm not sure how I got there or how much time had passed, yet there I was sitting quietly in the glider, moving back and forth, hair frazzled, clothes rumpled, with breakfast clinging to my once-white blouse.

Somehow, I find the strength to stand and survey the damage. The insurance adjuster in me proclaims the house a total loss. The Grandma in me smiles and remembers how much fun they had creating this disaster, how much I enjoyed watching them, and how much I was looking forward to their return.

Hell Night

Or Not So Rockin' New Year's Eve

by Betty Crow

For several years now, Dick Clark and a bottle of champagne have been my favorite way to spend New Year's Eve. There was a time when I took my life in my hands and actually went out, which is why when my daughter Julie asked to go to a New Year's Eve party, my immediate reaction was to say no. So, I did—for a minute or two. She wheedled, begged, and made promises until I finally gave in. After all, she was sixteen, and the party wouldn't require driving. She would be walking the two blocks to Amanda's house. The picture she painted seemed innocent enough, so I admonished her to be home by eleven o'clock and let her walk out the door.

Eleven o'clock came and went. Eleven thirty passed. I grabbed a jacket and went outside. No sign of daughter. I walked to her friend's house, where the party was allegedly held. Nothing. No lights, no music. I rang the bell, pounded on the door again and again, still no one answered. I gave the door a kick, hopped a few steps, and then stomped back home.

Midnight came and went. The people melted away from Times Square, leaving behind a mass of trash and debris. Still no daughter. I paced from the shiny white kitchen to the front door, peeked through the peep hole, hurried through the living room, and slowed my pace down the hallway. I checked to make sure she hadn't sneaked in through her window, which was unlikely since to do so would require the removal of a screen and the miraculous unlocking of a double lock. I checked anyway. After seven or eight similar tours, all the while belittling myself for being duped, I heard a noise on the front steps.

At first, I thought the sound was a dog scratching on the door. Then I heard Julie's house key hit the concrete. I looked at my watch. Two thirty-five a.m. As I listened to the scratching of the key on the lock, an angry red crept up my neck. Once I knew she was alive, my fear-tinged anger switched to full-on angry.

I crossed my arms and leaned back against the wall near the door to wait. I watched as the lock turned to the unlocked position and the door opened ever so slowly. I saw a head peek in through the crack in the door. When Julie saw me, she put a finger to her lips and said, “Shh, don’t wake mom. She’ll be mad.” I saw recognition dawn in her eyes. She tried to stand up straight, but tilted slightly left, as she staggered inside, “Hi Mom. Sho shorry I’m late.”

By now my anger was teetering on the edge of rage. I took hold of the front of Julie’s shirt and pulled her inside. After swinging her around and propping her against the wall, I slammed the door with my foot. My mouth opened, spewing forth a tirade of words and accusations, all the while pecking her in the chest with my pointer finger. With each poke, her head lolled from side to side, and the stupid grin on her face grew wider. I could see my rant wasn’t being heard, so I half dragged her down the hallway and tossed her on the bed. She bounced a few times and immediately fell asleep with that stupid grin still on her face. I thought back to a time when I came home in a similar condition. Luckily, I didn’t get caught. I looked down at my daughter, recognizing payback when I saw it.

Calm now, I brushed the hair from my baby’s eyes, pulled off her shoes, and tucked her into bed. I bent down to kiss that cute little nose and breathed a sigh of relief. She was home, and she was safe. As I left the room, I turned out the light, closed the door, and began planning the necessary consequences.

Oh Shit, I'm Late

The Other Side of the Story

"Just one more cup of punch, and then go home. It doesn't have that much vodka," urged Kelly.

I looked at my watch. It was another hour before curfew, so I reached for my refilled cup and took a sip, and then another. Kelly was right. I couldn't taste anything, so it wouldn't be like I was actually drinking. "Okay, but I can't be late. If mom finds out I'm here instead of at Amanda's, I'll be in big trouble."

The next time I looked at my watch the numbers were blurred. I asked Amanda to tell me the time, but she was asleep on the sofa. I would have asked Kelly, but she was asleep on the bathroom floor. She wasn't feeling well. I stumbled over something and banged my head against the wall. I wondered why it was so hard to walk. I finally found a clock on the kitchen wall. I panicked, "Oh shit, I'm late."

My efforts to hurry home failed. For some reason my feet felt heavy and my body tilted to the right. I couldn't walk straight. I lurched left, catching my foot on a crack in the sidewalk—or something. I stopped and tried to focus. After a block of stumbling, staggering, and lurching toward home, I gave up and sat down in the grass. I didn't feel well. I remembered Kelly was sick and decided it was probably something we ate.

Although my equilibrium was off, I finally found myself in front of the correct house. I dug in my pocket for the key and tried to find the keyhole. My hands were out of sync with my fingers, so I dropped the key. I finally found it and the keyhole. When the door opened, I peeked inside. I saw Brian standing there watching me. I put a finger to my lips and said, "Shh, don't wake mom. She'll be mad." When I recognized my error, I tried to stand up straight, tilting slightly left as I staggered inside. "Hi, Mom. Sho shorry I'm late."

What seemed like mere moments later, I heard the shrill sound of the alarm clock and felt a blinding pain in my head.

Undesirable Consequences

Julie's hand slammed down on the alarm. The red numbers said 5:30. She wasn't sure about a.m. or p.m. She intended to roll over and go back to sleep. A firm hand stopped her. She found herself sitting on the side of the bed, still fully dressed. Her head felt like an overly ripe watermelon splitting down the center.

With arms akimbo, Millicent glared at her daughter.

Picking up a pair of socks from the floor, Julie slipped

them over her cold feet and stood.

Millicent pointed toward the vacuum cleaner, plugged it in, and turned on the switch.

With one hand on her head in an effort to quell the pain and the other on the vacuum, Julie began a full morning of seemingly endless chores.

Millicent followed Julie around, making sure she kept moving, handing her dust cloths, mop buckets, scouring pads, and cleanser. There were no words of encouragement or assistance, only frowns.

Six long hours later, Julie found her mother in the kitchen. She tilted her head downward, smiled apologetically, and handed her mother a note.

Dear Mom, I'm sorry I came home late and for being a little under the weather. I knew the punch was spiked. I drank some even though I knew I shouldn't, but the other girls had some. I guess I drank too much. It made me sick. I'm so sorry. I promise never to be late again. Please don't be mad. Your loving daughter, Julie.

The Discussion

"I'm sorry, Mom."

"Do you understand why I'm angry?"

"Yes, but..."

"No buts. You were wrong to lie to me about where you

would be."

"But..."

"Don't interrupt me! You were out past your curfew."

"But..."

"You came home drunk!"

"Let me explain."

"Do you know how worried I was? You scared me. You could have been dead on the side of the road for all I knew."

"Mother, please let me explain."

"I'm listening."

"When I said I would be at Amanda's house, I thought that's where we were having our party. It wasn't until later that Amanda told me we were going to Kelly's. Kelly only lives another block down the street. I thought it would be okay."

"Why didn't you call?"

"I should have. We were busy making snacks to take with us. Anyway, once we got there, we started talking and drinking this delicious punch Kelly made. I didn't find out it contained alcohol until later. Her brother spiked it with vodka. Kelly said it didn't have much, and I believed her. We were having fun. We listened to music and talked, well until Kelly got sick and Amanda went to sleep."

"Went to sleep?"

"Okay—okay—passed out. In case you're wondering, I've learned my lesson. I promise never to drink again. My head is still pounding, and my stomach feels sick. I never want to feel like this again."

"You know there will be consequences."

"More than cleaning all morning?"

"Yes."

"What kind of consequences?"

"I'm not sure yet. I'll let you know when I decide. Now come here and let me give you a hug."

"I really am sorry, Mom."

"I know."

Mr. Muldoon Goes to Vegas

by Betty Crow

The television ads say, “What happens in Vegas, stays in Vegas.” Calvin was about to test truth in advertising. This was his first foray into the world since his wife Mae passed away last year. Their marriage lasted nearly forty years. It wasn’t all bliss, but for the most part, they were happy. Calvin loved his wife, mourned her, yet he was looking forward to kicking up his heels. After all, he was a single man.

Taking a vacation alone wasn’t a snap decision. At first, he thought about going to Porter Lake where he took Mae two years ago or to the mountains. But Calvin wanted to go somewhere new and different. His plan was to ditch all the widows who suddenly seemed to think he was Robert Redford. He craved excitement, and not the kind he would get watching Madeline and Bessie show him their boney, wrinkled knees. Madeline even went so far as to place her hand in a rather unexpected place during a game of bridge. Everyone thought Calvin was having a seizure. In reality, he was merely trying to avoid Madeline's curious exploration. His manic reaction was more than a little difficult to explain to the others, who insisted on calling the paramedics. Fortunately, he was able to dissuade them before Harvey actually dialed 9-1-1.

Calvin wouldn't have considered going to Las Vegas a mere six months ago. It was a decision made during a poker game at Walter's house. Calvin was having a streak of bad luck. He looked down at his poker hand. All small numbers. None matched. Bernard, Walter, and James were winning, Calvin was losing. He was down at least sixty cents. The cigar smoke made his eyes burn, and the beer tested his already-weak bladder. Calvin folded his pathetic cards, laid them on the table, and excused himself. On the way to the bathroom, he stopped in the living room to say hello to Effie, Walter's wife. The television was on. Effie was napping in her chair, so he didn't disturb her. It was then he saw the commercial: Dancing girls, bright lights, laughter, money, and bottomless cocktail glasses. Calvin raised a bushy eyebrow. Sinners! And the decision was made.

Picking up his carry-on bag, Calvin made his way

through the crowded airport. He bumped into a pretty brunette, nearly knocking her over. He grabbed her left arm and right breast, accidentally, to steady her. He smiled and said "I'm sorry" when he really wasn't. He might have been if it wasn't such a pleasurable experience. As he watched her walk away, Calvin tripped over a planter near the exit, causing him to stumble backward into a sunny, hot Nevada day.

Calvin looked for the shuttle to his hotel. He would be staying at the magnificent Peruvian Palace, a newly built monstrosity on the far side of the Luxor. He stepped into a rectangle marked off by yellow lines, stopped next to the Peruvian sign, and deposited his bag on the concrete. He waited as shuttle bus after shuttle bus came and went. None carried his hotel's insignia. A stretch limo stopped in front of him, blocking his view of the street. Calvin saw a shuttle bus pause beside the limo, but it kept going. He was beginning to think his choice in hotels wasn't so great, when an elegant, liveried man reached down to pick up his bag. He started to snatch it back. Understanding Calvin's suspicion, the driver asked, "Peruvian Palace?" The driver held the door while Calvin climbed into his luxury ride. Obviously, the Palace was a pretty swanky place.

After settling in for the ride to the hotel, Calvin

discovered he wasn't alone. Beside him was the most beautiful woman he had ever seen. She looked as if someone had taken Dolly Parton, stretched her into Gisele Bundchen, and sprinkled in a little Madonna attitude. And she was smiling at him. Not only was she smiling, she seemed to be offering him a glass of champagne. When Calvin didn't reach for the glass, the woman spoke, "Champagne, Mr. Mulder?"

"S-s-sure," Calvin said as he reached for the glass. Calvin's last name was really Muldoon, but he didn't correct her. He couldn't. He was too busy staring at the abundance of her…staring at the emerald pendant resting…he forced himself to ignore that freckle on her left…and looked up into smoky blue eyes. At that moment, he wished he looked more like Cary Grant than Rodney Dangerfield. Cary Grant wouldn't need words for a woman to fall in love with him, but since Calvin was no Cary, he was forced to come up with the perfect pick up line. Unfortunately, "Thank you," was all he could think of to say.

The woman leaned closer, resting her hand on his knee as she proceeded to speak in a low, Marilyn Monroe whisper, "So, Mr. Mulder, do you have a first name?"

"Calvin. Call me Calvin," he said, gulping his champagne, while leaning closer to the door. He unbuttoned the first button of his shirt and stretched his neck. He felt as if he were suffocating, in a good way.

"Hi Calvin, I'm Heather."

The breathy H sounds slipped through her lips, sending waves of warm breath to flutter lightly against his neck. He buttoned the first button of his shirt and shifted even closer to the door, all the time wondering who she was and why she acted as if he really were Cary Grant. He enjoyed Heather's attention, yet she was a little scary. She was even more forward than Madeline and Bessie.

Fortunately, the ride to the hotel was a short one. The limousine pulled up beneath the portico and a red-coated bellman came out to open the car door while the limo driver retrieved Calvin's bag from the trunk. Once Calvin and Heather were out of the car, the hotel bellman removed his hat and with an exaggerated flourish, bowed so deeply his head nearly touched the concrete. Calvin dug into his pocket and brought out two five-dollar bills. He handed one to the bellman, and one he exchanged for his bag. Curiously, the driver didn't seem to have a bag for Heather, and Heather didn't seem to have anywhere else to go. Instead of going inside to check in, she moved closer, slipping her right arm through his left, clinging to Calvin as if he belonged to her.

Heather didn't disappear until Calvin stopped at the back of the line for the front desk. He thought he was rid of her until he punched the elevator up button. That's when she reappeared, once again curled around his arm. Inside the elevator, Calvin punched the tenth-floor button and turned to Heather, "Which floor?"

Tipping her head to the side and giving him a slow wink, she said, "Ten is perfect."

Calvin checked the room number on his key card to the room numbers on the wall and turned right. Still clinging to Calvin's arm, Heather turned right as well. Calvin stopped, "What's your room number?"

Heather blinked slowly, "I'm in the room next to yours."

Calvin started walking again. His heart flipped over a time or two before he said, "Oh." Perhaps this was his lucky day.

After seeing Heather to her door, Calvin went to his room, which was far more luxurious than he would have imagined for a mere one hundred thirty dollars a night. There was a sunken living room with wall-to-ceiling windows which promised a magnificent view of the lights along Las Vegas Boulevard. The furnishings were right out of one of those home decorating magazines Mae always thumbed through at Home Depot. To his left were double doors leading into the bedroom. He wondered how he would be able to burrow beneath all the pillows propped up against the headboard. On the right was another set of double doors. These were locked. Calvin suspected they led to Heather's room. He raised one bushy eyebrow and then stopped his mind from going there, at least not right now. Right now, he had some gambling to do. "If you're going to sin, sin big," Calvin said as he took the one hundred-dollar bill he brought for gambling out of his wallet, kissed it, and set it next to his room key before heading for the shower.

After his shower, Calvin dressed in his best vacation outfit. He stood in front of the mirror, turned right, and then turned left. He liked the way the yellow and blue Hawaiian shirt matched his yellow walking shorts. He turned sideways and sucked in his rather rotund middle. *Maybe I'll go on a diet when I get home*, he thought. Calvin plopped a cream-colored Cabana hat on top of his head, smiled, and winked at himself in the mirror. He was ready.

After a leisurely dinner at the buffet, Calvin walked through the casino with his mouth open. Never had he seen such opulence or so many people in one place. He passed by the slots, the million-dollar machine, blackjack tables, finally coming to a stop in front of a roulette wheel.

This was his game. He could feel it. A man in a red jacket asked him to place his bet, but before he could, another red-jacketed man came up, whispered in the guy's ear, before turning his attention toward Calvin, "We have a private salon available. Follow me." Calvin followed.

Four hours later, Calvin was a little tipsy from all the free drinks but still winning. He lost a few times, but now he was up, way up. He couldn't believe how hot he was. No matter what number or color he called, that little ball hopped right in there. As far as his fuzzy brain could figure, he had about five hundred thousand of the casino's money. It was time to quit while he was ahead. He slugged down his last whisky sour and turned away from the table.

While his money was being exchanged, Heather made her appearance. "Well, aren't you the lucky one?" She snuggled up against Calvin's side, "I think you need to celebrate."

Calvin squeezed Heather against him, "I think you're right."

With her finger, Heather slowly traced the largest flower on his chest, while standing on her tiptoes to whisper in his ear, "You go on up to the room. I'll order some food and a bottle of champagne. I'll be right up. Don't start the party without me." She blew him a kiss and walked off. Calvin watched.

Calvin, his newly discovered ardor, and his winnings were escorted to his suite by security. The guards walked straight into the bedroom closet, opened the safe provided by the hotel, and placed the money inside. After giving Calvin the combination, they left.

Unsure as to whether he was supposed to wait inside his room or Heather's, he unlocked his side of the double doors and turned the knob. The doors opened. He decided she meant her room and went inside. Heather's bedroom was the mirror image of his. He sat down on the bed and leaned back against the mound of pillows. He adjusted himself to what he perceived to be his sexiest pose and settled in to wait for Heather.

He was about to doze off when the telephone rang. He almost answered it before he remembered this wasn't his room. The answering machine clicked on and he heard a male voice say, "The mark has the money. Mulder is the leak. You know what to do."

Calvin sat up. Was he the mark? Heather called him Mulder. Was she mispronouncing his name…or…how did she know his name anyway? Even the desk clerk thought he was Mr. Mulder and said his room was taken care of. At the time he thought the man meant from the credit card he used when making the reservations. Leak? Leak? They thought he was the leak. They were going to kill him.

Without another thought, Calvin went back to his room, carefully locking Heather's door behind him. He ran into the bedroom closet and opened the safe. After stuffing the money inside his travel bag, Calvin ran toward the door. As his hand reached for the knob, he heard a light tap on the door, "Honey, open up. It's little ol' me."

In a panic now, Calvin searched the room for another means of escape. He ran behind the sofa and looked outside. It was too far down to jump, but fortunately the building was an exact replica of early nineteen hundred architecture, which sported a fire escape. He unlatched the window and climbed out. Being careful to close the window behind him, he took off down the stairs. By the time he reached the street, he was gasping for breath. He feared having a heart attack and dying before he could spend a penny of his winnings.

Calvin stumbled around the corner and found refuge behind a row of shrubs. He sat down to catch his breath. He tensed when he heard running footsteps and Heather's voice, "He'll be on the next flight to Boston. Let's go."

After the car squealed off into the night, Calvin hailed a cab, "Greyhound bus station please."

Six months later

What happened in Vegas, did stay in Vegas. Calvin religiously read the Boston papers, eventually seeing William Mulder's obituary. It seems Mr. Mulder was found floating in the Charles River. Apparently, he slipped while fishing along the riverbank and drowned.

Calvin was happy to be back in Phoenix. He no longer felt the need to travel, alone or otherwise. He was happy to spend time with friends and play bridge. Instead of having a seizure, Calvin winked at Madeline and smiled as her roving hand found his thigh. He decided wrinkled boney knees weren't so bad after all.

Small Town Saturday Night

by Betty Crow

Birds flit back and forth, hurrying to bring home one last worm for their babies. A warm breeze rustles the leaves of a nearby maple tree. A teenager drives by in his freshly polished pickup truck, windows down, music thumping. One car drives slowly down Main Street. The man has white hair, as does his wife. They wave; I wave back. A young couple is walking through the alley, pushing their baby in a stroller. Their son rides his bicycle alongside. They wave; I wave back. Everyone knows everyone here. It's a small-town Saturday night.

Since my house is on a corner lot, I'm entertained by the comings and goings on both Main and Harrison streets, as well as the alley. The deck offers shelter from the bright evening sun, while providing a view of the newly planted butterfly bush and flourishing tomato plants. Water drips from freshly watered pansies in the window box next to me.

Droplets collect on their upturned faces, emphasizing the already bright yellows, dark reds, and deep purples. The grill is cooling after providing a tasty dinner of steak and potatoes. The meal is finished, the kitchen tidy, and the coffee is ready for the morning. After checking to see if there might actually be anything good on television, I retire to the deck with a glass of red wine.

A newly graduated teenager stops by to say hello. He has a summer job working for his father. He will start classes at the community college in the fall. His older brother leaves for Iraq in a few weeks. He seems worried, but proud. He doesn't visit long. He's on his way to pick up his girlfriend. They're going to one of the few remaining drive-in movie theaters, twenty miles away, to see the new Indiana Jones movie.

The sun sinks below the horizon. The streetlights come on, illuminating a street lined with signs bearing yellow ribbons with the names of hometown boys serving in the military. One has given his life for our freedom. The community prays for him and prays for all the other boys to come back safe.

Those who make it home are treated like royalty. A banner hangs over the street welcoming Joshua home. He will arrive tomorrow, escorted by the town's fire truck and only police car. Their sirens will announce his arrival. Residents will flock to the sidewalks to wave, and he will wave back. Everyone is thankful he made it home safe.

The low moan of a train whistle breaks the silence. I listen to the bumping of the cars as the train stops, takes off, and stops again. When it starts moving, the whistle echoes through the night as it approaches the first railroad crossing and then another. I think it's leaving, but then the cars banging together tell me there are more cars to add. It reverses. When the engine passes under a streetlight, I see it is the red train, not the black one. The red train never leaves the switching yard. It only moves cars around on the many rows of tracks. As the train gets longer, and each time it takes off down the tracks, I make silent bets on whether it's leaving or if it will reverse again. It becomes a game. Two hours later I'm still playing. I call it a night.

Through the open bedroom window, I hear crickets chirping. A dog barks, another answers, and then another. Two cats are squaring off next door, their low yowls warn of the fight to come. The train's whistle moans one last time as it picks up speed. This time it doesn't reverse.

I closed my eyes, opened them, and sat up. *Next weekend is the Betsey Reed re-enactment. Who was Betsey Reed anyway?* I wondered. And then I remembered she was hung for poisoning her husband. I remembered seeing a book in the window of the library down the street. I smacked my pillow into shape, snuggled down for the night, and thought *I'll buy one.*

Next weekend, I will invite a friend to go to the Betsey Reed Festival. After the festival, I will probably cook dinner on the grill, and we will sit outside on the back deck. We'll talk about our week, solve the problems of the world, and tell stories from when we were young. When neighbors wave as they pass by, we'll wave back. It will be another exciting small-town Saturday night. To those used to the faster pace of city life, my weekends may seem dull. To me, they're priceless.

The Abandoned Tree

by Betty Crow

It would be the first Christmas post-divorce. Brian was twelve years old and Tami was ten. I worked for Blue Cross in Richardson, Texas, making a mere whisper over a pittance. Needless to say, finances were tight. There wasn't enough money for both a tree and presents. I decided to make sure my kids had presents and explained to them we wouldn't be putting up a tree. They took the news in stride, seemingly unaffected by what I felt was devastating news. Knowing how much I enjoyed colorful Christmas lights, they were more concerned about me than themselves.

Christmas Eve afternoon, I was busy folding laundry when I heard my daughter's excited voice. I looked outside and saw her dragging pieces of an artificial Christmas tree through the back gate. I went outside to see what was going on.

Running toward me with a wide smile on her face, she called, “Look, mom! I found a Christmas tree.”

Skeptical as to where she might have “found” this tree, I asked where she got it.

“Someone threw it away. It was in a garbage can down the back alley.”

I reached for the tree, inspecting its remains. It was a little worse for wear, certainly ready for the trash, but I could see the pride in my daughter’s face. She would be disappointed if I rejected her gift.

“Go find your brother, and we’ll put up our Christmas tree,” I said.

The finished tree was approximately five feet high. The only problem—there were gaping holes where greenery should have been. Several branches were missing. Tami went back down the alley where she found the tree, but couldn’t find the elusive pieces.

“No problem,” I said. “We’ll use the branches from the back to fill in the holes and hide the bare side of the tree in the corner.”

That tree was the scrawniest, most bedraggled tree I have ever seen—barely better than Charlie Brown’s tree. Yet, it was almost pretty after a few boxes of tinsel, ornaments, and three strings of lights. Once we were finished decorating, we stood back to admire our handiwork.

That night, after Brian plugged in the lights, the tree's defects seemed to magically disappear. I looked down at the pride on my daughter's face and knew I would never forget that moment. Even though we didn't have money for a fancy tree, expensive presents, or a table filled with goodies, we were blessed with a special Christmas memory to cherish in our hearts forever. It's one of those stories we still drag out and dust off when we are all together. With each laughter-filled telling that poor abandoned tree gets smaller, uglier, and more bedraggled, yet that Christmas became one of our most cherished memories.

The Betsey Reed Festival

by Betty Crow

The newspaper headline read, “Betsey Reed Fest Promises Tacky and Tasteless Fun.” If I could, I would have danced a jig. Come on, Friday night! The two-day festival would have street music, crafts, food vendors, and wine tasting.

And as if that wasn’t enough, Friday night there was to be a free showing of *Arsenic and Old Lace* outside in the street. If you’re not older than dirt or a true movie buff, you may not remember this one. It’s a Frank Capra film starring Cary Grand, I mean Grant. Mortimer, played by the hunky Mr. Grant, visits two aunts who seem to have developed a penchant for serving arsenic laced elderberry wine.

What does *Arsenic and Old Lace* have to do with Betsey Reed? Betsey was accused of using a little arsenic to poison her husband. He died. She was convicted of murder. Since the movie couldn’t begin until after dark, the

Fife Opera House would begin the evening with a re-enactment of the hanging of Betsey Reed. It would be a fun-filled evening, followed by more unusual events on Saturday.

For those of you who don't know about Elizabeth (Betsey) Reed, which included me before this event, in 1845 she was the first woman to hang in the State of Illinois. She was also the *only* woman hanged in the state. Some thought she might be innocent. Still, she was accused and convicted. Many residents of the town thought she was a witch. Why? Because while Betsey was incarcerated in the Palestine jail, it caught fire and burned to the ground. She was suspected of doing the deed. Of course, since she didn't have matches, she must have used her evil powers.

After the fire, Betsey was moved to the jail in Lawrenceville. The day of Betsey's hanging, thousands of people gathered to watch the publicly proclaimed witch and murderer as she rode from the jail to the noose atop a casket made especially for her. Without further ado, Betsey was hanged by the neck until dead.

My heart beat excitedly, as I looked at the clock that Friday afternoon. Five more minutes and my work week would be done. This was the first day of the Betsey Reed Festival. My friend Judy, visiting from Pennsylvania, was here to go with me. With a flick of a wrist and a flourish of hands, I cleared off my desk, told my cohorts goodbye, and practically skipped to the car. I drove as fast as I could, without getting a speeding ticket, and arrived home in record time.

After a quick change into my festival clothes, I grabbed Judy by the arm, and practically dragged her out the door. Since the festival would take place right in front of the house, we didn't have far to go. At the end of our sidewalk, we stopped. We looked up and down the street for the tents. There were only four tents set up along the entire length of our block. Before I could ask why, there was a flash of lightening, immediately followed by the loud rumble of thunder and torrential rain. We ran back inside.

We watched from the living room window, as festival-goers and vendors alike scrambled for cover. The wind blew the trees until I thought they would break in half. We turned on the TV to see if there were severe storms in the area. The electricity flashed off, back on, and off again. It was then the warning sirens began to scream. My teeth started chattering, but not because I felt a chill. My teeth chattered because of my past experiences with tornadoes. I was downright scared.

Judy helped me gather a few supplies. We found a

lantern and flashlights and placed them, along with two lawn chairs, beside the basement door. We were ready to run for cover, but we decided to tempt fate. We listened as hail pelted the roof and rain flew sideways against the house. We waited, but we didn't hear that distinctive roar, so we remained upstairs. The rain continued to pour down, not little pitter pats, but in buckets and barrels. The electricity came back on, so we watched the warnings scroll by: tornado, severe thunderstorm, and then flood.

After a full night of very little sleep, we woke to a bright sunshiny Saturday. I breathed a sigh of relief. Certain the festival would go on as planned, I bounded out of bed looking forward to a day of fun and excitement. Judy poured each of us a cup of coffee and turned on the TV. I groaned. The Wabash River had left its banks. The massive rain flooded creeks, overflowing even the smallest streams. During the night, our little town had become an island.

Worried the festival was cancelled, while still in my robe, I ripped open the front door. I ran down the front walk, skidded to a stop, reversed, ran back inside, and slammed the door. Right in front of the house, a barbecue restaurant just happened to be firing up the grill. In spite of my embarrassment, there was a little hop in my step as I headed for the shower. The festival would take place as scheduled despite the rain. It was time to P-A-R-T-Y! Judy was ready before me. She waited patiently while I worried over what to wear, slapped on a little makeup, and tried to tame untameable hair. I avoided the mirror as I passed by. Judy made the appropriate complimentary remarks and held the door open for me. I guess she was tired of waiting.

At the end of our sidewalk, I stopped and looked both ways. The barbeque vendor was still there, but there were no vendors to the north and very few to the south. I saw an artist hawking wooden roses across the street. We stopped in front of the tent to admire the blue, red, and yellow varieties. They were nice, but merely dust catchers to me. We continued down the street, looking for food and finally decided on a pork chop on a stick. Yum! We stood in the shade of a building while we ate, licked our fingers clean, and then went in search of a trash receptacle. There were no more tents, but there were a few show cars to admire. We did. Now what? It seemed the flood water had marred my fun after all.

Judy said, “I saw a sign about a wine tasting inside the Fife Opera House.”

“Now you’re talking,” I said.

It seems the wine vendors were required to sign in the

night before. We were in luck. The Fife Opera House was filled with booths from every winery in the Central Illinois area. We each handed a lady $10.00 in exchange for an empty wine glass, and then proceeded to the first booth. We chose a fine red wine, sipped, rolled it around on our tongues, and swallowed, as if we knew what we were doing. We made the appropriate euphoric facial expressions and moved on to the next booth where we repeated our performance. And so on, and so on, until my little teetotaler-self could hardly see through the fog. Perhaps teetotaler isn't quite the right word. After all, I do drink occasionally but usually not more than one or two glasses of wine in an evening. If I should have more, I'm under the table. I was on the verge of under but still wobbling along, when I gave Judy the "let's get out of here" look. Realizing her friend was a little tipsy, she obliged.

"You look like you could use some fresh air," she said.

Back in the street, someone had lined up what appeared to be soap box derby cars, yet they were different than any I'd seen before. These cars had a handle on the back, like a grocery cart. All were painted bright colors and positioned at an angle in the middle of the street.

"Is there a soap box derby?" I slurred quizzically.

"No. I heard a lady say they are built for the casket

races."

These were not what I envisioned when I first heard the term casket races. In my mind's eye, there would be wooden caskets built like the ones on Gunsmoke, with six pallbearers carrying a pretend deceased person lying prone on top. I think my version would be more fun. The race was to begin at eleven, but it was cancelled, so I missed out. Bummer!

We crossed the street. I tripped on the curb and almost knocked down a sign advertising a book about Betsey Reed. I decided to buy one. While Judy was conversing with someone she knew but I didn't, I careened through a group of festival goers blocking the sidewalk and grabbed hold of a post in front of the book store.

Since I knew a little more about Betsey Reed, the name on the window had a whole new meaning. It's called Betsey Reed's Book Emporium. Below the name it says, a great place to hang around. I had passed that bookstore many times, wishing it were open during evening hours or on Saturday. I guess I thought Betsey owned the store. The owner is actually a man named Rick Kelsheimer, who penned the book The Hanging of Betsey Reed, a Wabash River Tragedy on the Illinois Frontier.

Inside the store, I found myself all alone. I located a copy of the book and picked up another by one of my favorite authors. I looked around for someone to take my money, but there wasn't another soul around. As I was about to put my books back and leave, a man walked in. He introduced himself as the author. He signed my book, and we talked for a while. I tried not to slur, but I'm not sure I succeeded. He explained the payment procedure. It seems locals know to take their money next door to the art gallery. Since I've only lived here a few months, I wasn't aware of this practice. Small towns, you gotta love 'em!

Back outside, I found Judy still talking to the same guy. I motioned her over to where a wooden casket had been propped against the wall. She stood beside it while I took a picture. We joked about my measuring her to see if she would fit. She said she would be doing all the cooking for the remainder of her visit. No chance of arsenic poisoning for her.

I told Judy I thought it would be best if I went back inside until my wine-fuzzed brain de-fuzzed. She agreed. I went home, swallowed a pain reliever to stave off an impending headache, and fell asleep.

A while later, Judy woke me to say the street dance had been cancelled. She wanted to know if I wanted to spend $16.00 to watch the WrestleMania show instead. It didn't take me long to decline. We stood outside, talked to a few neighbors, and watched the wrestlers pass by on their way to the ring. Talking with friends was much more fun than watching wrestlers, plus we each saved $16.00.

Later we decided to sit outside on the deck. We talked about the day. Judy said she was sorry the flood had ruined the festival. I explained the festival was moved up a few weeks this year to avoid hot weather. We decided it would have been better to be hot than flooded.

Even though I didn't get to experience the usual Betsey Reed Festival, I saw enough to realize the newspaper article was correct. This festival did provide plenty of "tacky and tasteless" fun. I'm already looking forward to next year when the street will be lined with tents and all events will go off as planned. Hopefully, we won't hear the high-pitched scream of tornado sirens and there won't be another flood. Next time, I want to see a casket race.

The Face in the Window

by Betty Crow

Hugs were something other mothers gave their children. Mine didn't readily show affection, yet I felt her love all around me. It wasn't until my mother was in her seventies that I took it upon myself to give her a hug and speak the words out loud, "I love you, Mom." After that, hugs and saying I love you became the norm. It felt so good to hug and be hugged, that I often wondered why I hadn't made the effort sooner.

I was a working, single mother and money was often tight. Vacations were usually a quick trip home for Thanksgiving and some years, a week during the summer. I lived in Texas—Mom lived in Illinois.

Each year the lines seemed to grow deeper, and the light in her eyes appeared dimmer. Time had etched its mark on her face, slowed her movements, and taken away her ability to see well enough to enjoy quilting—her favorite pastime. I didn't like seeing her frailties. They made me too aware of her mortality.

It was the Sunday after Thanksgiving 1998. The car was loaded, and I was heading back to Dallas. Before I walked out the door, I turned to give my mom a hug.

"I love you."

"I love you, too," she said. "Be careful."

I settled myself in the driver's seat and put the car in reverse. As the car moved backward, tears seeped from my eyes, splashing onto the front of my Dallas Cowboy's sweatshirt. I wished I could have stayed longer, spent more time with my mom. I wouldn't see her again until spring, and I would miss her.

The car came to a stop in front of the house. It was time to drive down the road that would put seven-hundred-fifty miles between us, yet I couldn't shift gears. Through the dim morning light, my eyes searched until they found her face in the window. I waved goodbye, she waved back, both crying, both smiling through our tears, both blissfully unaware it was the last time.

Photo supplied by author

ABOUT ELSIE MARIE MEDCALF GEORGE

Elsie Marie George is youngest of 8 Medcalf children. All

love music and writing. Brothers Richard and Ollie, and sister Lena are published poets. Brother Robert writes poems and gospel songs.

One of Elsie's poems won second place in the 2020 writers' contest, and one of her short stories won first place in the 2019 contest. Two of her poems were read at her elementary school and high school graduations. She wrote newsletters, writes gospel songs, and continues to write short stories which are published in Bristow News under "Family Discussions."

A Fifth Dan Black Belt, she taught Life Skills and wrote short stories about virtue and character development for her students in TaeKwon-Do for 23 years. She is currently employed at Bristow Library and leads the weekly "Ms. Elsie's Storytime" program.

She graduated from Tulsa University *Summa Cum Laude* with a Bachelor of Science in double majors Philosophy and Psychology where she contributed to Dr. Robert Hanson's study and publication in *Family Living.* Awards include: Salutation in Ahloso Elementary School; special awards in Stonewall High School scholastics, music, and basketball; softball; BPW Club; trophies and medals in martial arts including Oklahoma State Champion in patterns.

Elsie took part in archaeological excavations as a vocational archaeologist; taught 7 years in Bristow Early Head Start; plays guitar and piano, and tries her hand at ukulele, mandolin, autoharp, dulcimer, psaltry, and melodian.

Elsie states: “I may not be as loquacious as my siblings, but I

believe people need to express thoughts to uplift others. Written word and music offer inspiration and growth in wisdom and understanding.”

2nd Place Winner

Valentine's Day Poetry Contest

First Embrace

Oh, the years have slipped away so fast!
Our love has not diminished. We first embraced
Only yesterday, it seems. You sighed for our touch to last.
You felt my love for you which I had not faced.
That's how it began, our life together. To this day
Your caress delights me still. My hand you hold
Each time we walk together. "I love you," still you say.

Each embrace echoes the first as I your arms enfold.
I don't know how I could return to just "I," from our "we."
Peace and belonging are things I feel with you.
Your love is my treasure; you are precious to me.
Before our embrace, loneliness was what I knew.
So, on this Valentine Day, My Love, I pray
God grants you health and joy and peace.
May our love only deepen with each day,
Until our first embrace in Heaven, when days here cease.

Dilemma

by Elsie Marie Medcalf George

Marie had just pulled up to the church parking lot to let her six-year old son Barrett attend the youth program when she noticed a group of older teenage boys gathered on the sidewalk across the street from the church. Taking a closer look, she saw that two boys were fighting, and the other boys formed a circle around the fighters. Without thinking about what she might do, she said, “Stay in the car,” and hurried across the street. By the time she had arrived at the scene, on of the fighters had been knocked to the sidewalk and the other was standing over him. The group of boys surrounding the fighters were urging the fight to continue. Marie saw that there was blood on the boy’s head and on the sidewalk where he lay. The sight of the blood caused her to think that this could be a very serious injury which might mean disaster for both of these young boys.

Not considering her safety, she stepped into the circle of

boys, looked at the standing fighter and calmly said, “Cool it, man.” The fighter’s eyes looked glazed and far away. The other boys were telling her she had no business interfering, but she kept looking into the fighter’s eyes and calmly addressed him, saying, “You can stop now, can’t you?” Slowly, the young man’s eyes focused on her and he turned and walked away.

By that time, a schoolteacher had arrived and was talking to the boys. The one on the sidewalk got up and as he turned to walk away, he looked back at Marie, then continued on his way. Marie returned to the car and began to violently shake in the aftermath of released tension. “Dddon’t yyyou ever do what I jjjust did!” she told her son. “That was not sssafe!”

Barrett thought about what he had just witnessed. His one-hundred-and-five-pound mother had broken up a fight between muscular teenage boys by talking! She could have been hurt if the standing fighter had not regained control of himself. What if she had not interfered? It created a dilemma in her your son’s mind. What was the right thing to do?

3rd Place Winner

Short Story Contest

A Measure of Faith

by Elsie Marie George

My brother Robert lives his fain in God's mercy and grace through music. As a teenager he was song leader at out church and sang with our father in a quartet. All his life, in every church which he attended, he was song leader. Throughout his lifetime, he memorized many hymns. Robert also wrote numerous gospel songs and sang some of them in his church. He could pick out songs on the piano, and he played harmonica. Robert felt that his life's calling was glorifying God with music.

In later years, he had heart surgery. During the operation he suffered a stroke which left him mostly bind. He could barely see out of one eye. I visited him while he was in rehab. When I entered the dining room, he was sitting at a table preparing for lunch, and he was praying. After his prayer, I greeted him. He said, “All is for God’s glory.” Several of our family were also there and wanted to help him, but he insisted on doing things as much by himself as possible. One of my sisters asked him about a song, in order to gauge his memory function. He treated us to a lovely song of praise.

During recovery, he confessed it was not easy because he felt if he could not continue music in the church, he was not fulfilling God’s purpose for his life. He was told his vision would not improve. He received new glasses and was able to walk unassisted in familiar and some unfamiliar places.

None of the family stopped praying for his complete recovery. He improved, and once again led songs by memory in his church. If there was a song of which he was unsure, his loving and loyal wife Sylvia would help him memorize it, measure by measure.

To honor him, I wrote a song:

"As he sat at the table, he scarce could see a thing.
Still he prayed, still he prayed.
He said, 'All is for God's glory' and a sweet song he did sing.
Still he praised, still he praised.

(chorus)
He said, "I'll praise the Lord at all times;
I will always speak his praise.
I will boast only in his love for me.
Come let us tell together the wonders of his grace,
For from my fear, He has set me free."

(verse 2)
As I gazed on my brother, and pondered at his faith,
Sorrow eased; sorrow eased.
There's no limit to God's mercy, no boundary to his grace.
I felt joy; I felt peace.

(chorus)
"And I will praise the Lord at all times,

I will always speak His praise.
I will boast only in His love for me.
Come let us tell together the wonder of his grace
For from out fear, He has set us free."

Trust

by Elsie Marie George

I was only four years old when I learned how to swim. Being the youngest of eight children. I tried to do what my older siblings did. That was why I wanted to swim. My older brothers Ollie and Robert were lifeguards at the swimming pool which our father managed at Double Lakes. We swam every day during the summer months. I especially enjoyed a game Ollie and I played before I learned to swim. I would walk out onto the adult diving board. When Ollie called, "Jump!" I would jump into his arms into the deep water where he would catch me and swim with me back to the edge of the pool.

Years later when I was around ten years old, my brother Richard and I were walking along the railroad track near our home, as we often did when either hiking or returning from church services just one-quarter mile away. We walked out onto the trestle. We were about halfway to the other side of the trestle when we stopped. I saw a tiny yellow dandelion growing between the wooden planks on the trestle and that intrigued me enough to stop and wonder how it got there. Richard was looking down into the deep ravine below us when suddenly we became aware of the train barreling down the railroad tracks toward us!

"Run!" yelled Richard, and he ran along the trestle and made it safely to the other side. Since I was smaller, I was afraid to fun for fear that my feet would get caught between the wooden planks or that I would fall. I walked as quickly as I could. When I was still about twenty feet away from the end of the trestle, Richard yelled, "Jump!" I jumped off the railroad track and into the arms of my big brother. And the train roared by where I had been just seconds before!

Building trust does not always come from such dramatic episodes as ours. Sometimes it is just conditioning from being able to rely on people who are always there when you need them ... such as my brothers.

To My Sister, Lena Mae

by Elsie Marie Medcalf George

Mother's face was like mine—the eyes, the nose,
the brow.
But I did not know her and do not know her now.
Still, I must know something of her in Sister's
gentle ways:
The answers soft, the loving hand, the words of praise.
Only Mother could have made herself thus known
By giving to Sister her love seeds sown
Into such a willing heart; such hands that uplift
And care for others because of Mother's gift.
Since by the fruit it bears, a tree can be known,
I surely see in Sister Mother's love seeds sown.

ABOUT EVA HARTLEY

Eva Hartley, a relatively new writer, reaches into her own life experiences and writes from the heart. She attributes growth in writing to her writer friends in the Ada area who have been a constant source of encouragement.

Her first "published" work was the dedication in her 1970 school annual. Since then she has been published in Creations 2018 and Creations 2019. She has found her niche in writing what she calls her "little bitty ditties," commonly known as Haiku.

In addition to her writing, Eva enjoys painting, gardening, and joining friends in attending Ada Writers, Writing for Fun, and Daughters of the Revolution, when not isolated because of the COVID-19 pandemic.

A native New Mexican, she was reared by hard working cotton farmers who lived close to the earth in a minimalist fashion. She attributes her "small" writing to this upbringing. Eva has made Oklahoma her home for 36 years and lives a rich life with her husband, Billy, and their three dogs, on a spread in rural Pottawatomie county.

Layers

Civilizations

Old and new laid on the Earth

Know not of each other

By Eva Hartley

Jonah Season

Where are you my muse?

Darkness is crushing my soul

Must discover God

by Eva Hartley

Rx

A call to loving

Unite the Earth with love

Watch it heal itself

By Eva Hartley

Desert Monsoons

Thunderheads building

Growing larger by the day

At last, the rain pours

By Eva Hartley

Church

No fellowship there

Smiling faces, insincere

A disappointment

By Eva Hartley

Dark

It haunts me nightly

Embarrassing memory

My body shudders.

By Eva Hartley

Too Late

My wretched soul cries

For a chance to live my life

But Father Time laughs

By Eva Hartley

Honesty

My words betray me

Offering clues to my heart

Enemies slay me

By Eva Hartley

Hubs

He knows just one way

My job is to support him

While my ways die out

By Eva Hartley

Eyesight

I see not myself

Others evaluate me

And press me down hard

By Eva Hartley

Winner of the

Water-Ways Haiku and Poetry

Contest

Dam

Stone blocking cold creek

Mans bridge to natures wonder

White water cascades

By Eva Hartley

Winner of the

Water-Ways Haiku and Poetry

Contest

Pole Fishing

Concentric circles

Water waves nudging bobber

Elusive supper

By Eva Hartley

ABOUT SUSAN HARVEY

Susan Harvey began writing with no previous writing experience, at the age of seventy-three. An avid reader, writing is something she has always considered but never tried. She plunged in with both feet, joining Ada Writers and Writing for fun, two writing groups in Ada, Oklahoma.

She enjoys writing about what she knows from her own experiences and observations of life. She has been published in Creations 2019 and Creations 2020. She is serving as the current secretary of Ada Writers.

Susan is a retired registered nurse and continues to use her nurse's training in local private homes. She keeps a busy schedule, volunteering in her church, the food pantry and more to assist the needy. This year she invited several homeless women to stay at her house when the COVID-19 pandemic shut down local shelters.

She is the mother of two, grandmother of five, and great-grandmother of five. If that isn't enough, she also enjoys caring for her two dogs and four cats. She loves animals. She delights in music, dance, and theater, always in a rich gathering of friends.

The Snowball Tree

by Susan Harvey

I heard the phone ring, waking me just enough to hear Daddy say, “Yello” then,“No you don’t need to come today. I forgot about that. If you really want to be here, I will come pick you up as soon as I get the pick-up out of the driveway. Okay till then.”

Mother came in the kitchen, “Who was that?”

“It was Mrs. Whitehead. She says she promised John she would be here for his birthday and make a special cake.”

“Yes, I heard all about it. I really need to go to the office. Do you want me to drive or do you want to take me” Mother said?

“I’ll take you then swing by and get her. What’s your plan?”

“I need to get the statements out before the end of the month,” she said.

"Don't stay all day it's only going to get worse as the day goes along."

"OK, till noon I think," Mother said.

The wind howled and then I heard the radio, saying that the schools are closed today! That got me out of bed in a hurry. I ran to the kitchen and said. "Is it true? We don't have to go to school?"

"Yes, you could go back to sleep if you want, but don't wake up John yet. I want the big boys to shovel me out of the driveway first," said Daddy.

"We got that much snow?" I ran to the den and looked out the 'picture window'. The snow was falling heavily and starting to really pile up. *That will be so much fun.* I went to get dressed and see if John had awakened. He was gone to the world. *That's okay I will watch my big brothers shovel the snow without him.*

The older boys were in high school now and Daddy had them do a lot of chores around the house. He went to wake them up and they thought they had to go to school, but he asked them to get their boots on so they could shovel the snow from the driveway.

Slowly they dragged out of bed and mother had some breakfast for them. That got them going. They headed outside. I watched them from the big window in the dining room. Daddy wouldn't let me go out till they finished. So, I changed windows when they went to the front of the house.

Finally, John got up and had his pancakes about the time the boys came in from the snow. Mother made them go to the back door so they wouldn't make a mess. They said it wasn't really cold yet if you weren't in the wind. Daddy told them to stay home while

Photo supplied by author

he took Mother to the office and picked up Mrs. Whitehead.

They too were eager to get out and get their car on the

road. There was a bit of grumbling. They both went off to call friends while Daddy was gone. I sat with John and watched him eat. He was so slow! We had all kinds of plans to get outside.

When Daddy returned, he let Whitehead out and helped her to the door. She was our housekeeper since John was a baby. We loved her so much. We didn't call her Mrs. Whitehead, just 'Whitehead'. She was like a grandmother. She raised eight children of her own and was a widow. The ideal caretaker.

After a few cartoons we finally got to go outside. The snow was up to my knees and a little more on John. The boys decided to clear off the front walks and the porch so they could bring some friends over. In the front an elm tree had lost a small limb. They started to drag it to the back, but John said he wanted it for a tree. They made a pile and planted the limb in it so it wouldn't fall over. John was satisfied. He started making snowballs and cupping them around the branches.

When I asked him what he was doing he said, "I am making a snowball tree for my birthday."

I laughed so hard I started rolling in the snow. The older boys went for the camera and took pictures of John with his snowball tree so we would always have it. That was the highlight of the morning. Mother and Daddy were impressed with his ingenuity

Photo provided by author

ABOUT AVIS HUDSON

Avis Hudson entered Ada Writer's Valentine's Day Poetry Contest and won first place! She lives in Asher, Oklahoma.

1st Place Winner

Valentine's Day Poetry Contest

My Field

by Avis Hudson

In my youth my Father gave unto me a field.

Though difficult the furrows to hoe.

Great bounty with glorious beauty was my yield.

Into the eternal storehouse it will go.

Thank you, Father, for the field I tilled

And the seeds I sow.

ABOUT RICHARD MEDCALF

Richard Medcalf started writing poetry at the age of 16. His poems have been published in several magazines, chapbooks, anthologies and newspapers, quoted by ministers, gospel radio and television programs. His poetry has been set to music and he has won many contests. He has appeared in Ada Writers Creations 2016–2017–2018–2019 and now 2020.

He is a man for all seasons who loves to hunt, fish and play golf. He had one “hole-in-one” in golf. He scored 289 in bowling and missed a perfect game because a wobbly tenpin did not fall in the second frame, even though he had strikes the rest of the game. He loved fast pitch softball and was a catcher in the Marine Corps intramural league and caught for 25 years in Texas.

He lives in Oklahoma now with his wife Wanda. He lives by the Code of The Corps: Honor, Courage, Commitment. “Once a Marine always a Marine.”

Asleep at the Wheel

by Richard Medcalf

She was strapped in her seat
as I drove down the road.
The radio played
good old country songs.

As she slept in her seat
there by my side,
I knew I would ask her
to please be my wife.

Thinking of things
that one day might be
if she would say, “yes,”
she would marry me.

I slowly dozed off
as I drove home that night.
Asleep at the wheel,
I cost her her life

Bowling

by Richard Medcalf

Back in my middle age—about my fifties, I guess—I decided to start bowling with some of my co-workers during our one-hour lunch break. We were just practicing, but we all liked it enough, so I started talking to them about bowling in a league.

We were all about average, but we decided to check into it. We found out it would be a mixed league, so we needed a woman to bowl with us.

During our noon practice, we had seen a young woman bowling by herself who was pretty good, so we asked her to bowl with us. She said, "Okay." Her name was Cat.

We needed a team name, so I suggested, "Three Hounds and a Fox." They all liked it.

The first year we bowled, we won the league, and we were excited. I was the anchor with the 181 average. The next year, I wasn't doing as well, and I only had a 165 average. We had a chance to win the league again, and with my last ball, I needed three pins for us to win. But when I laid the ball down on the lane, it scooted straight into the gutter. I knew I had put it down in the right place,so I couldn't figure out what happened until I retrieved my ball and found a grease spot on it. One of the other team's members had put it there. So, we came in second.

We were all disappointed, of course.

During that year I had bowled a 289, which was almost a perfect game of 300. In the second frame the tenpin wobbled around but finally fell, so even though I struck out all the other frames, I missed my perfect game.

We had a lot of fun and met some good friends, but I'll always be a little disappointed in myself for not winning the league and not bowling a perfect game.

One good thing, though, is that I met my wife Wanda there at the bowling alley, and we've been married for 18 years.

It Might Have Been

by Richard Medcalf

When life seems sad and lonely,
There's nothing you can do.
You wish you had someone to love,
Someone to tell your troubles to.

You reminisce about the past,
And your eyes fill up with tears.
The joys and heartaches that you've shared,
Will last a thousand years.

There's always "Someone Special"
Who stole your heart away.
You thought she loved you very much,
But then she left one day.

Now her memory just won't die.
Her lips, her hair, her eyes.
I still see them in my dream.
I still see them in my mind.

Looking back in time, my dear,
I still keep looking back at you.
I recall the happiness and love that we shared then,
And I recall that old quotation:
"The saddest words of tongue or pen are
these four words:
"It might have been."

It's Time

by Richard Medcalf

When I came home last night,
There was a slight smell of cigar in the air.
I don't smoke, so I knew it shouldn't be there.

I heard the tension in your voice.
I knew something was very wrong.
I thought of the fussing and fighting
That's been going on.

Then I saw a ring and watch on the tabletop.
I knew that it was time.
For when you woke up this morning,
You whispered his name instead of mine.

Memories of Love

by Richard Medcalf

Through the shadows of my mind,
Flash the traces of our life.
Flicking images of me and you,
Of all the things we used to do.

We walked together hand in hand,
Our hearts chained together by a golden wedding band
A kiss, a hug, or just a little touch.
When you're in love with each other
,
These things mean so much.
They strengthen your heart,
And give you peace of mind.
Just holding each other
For the rest of your lifetime.

For two people together,
Give strength to each other.
And love conquers all,
As one shares with the other.
We walked together hand in hand,
Our hearts chained together by a golden wedding band

My Deer Hunting Trip

by Richard Medcalf

When I was 18 and finished with high school, my dad decided it was time for me to leave home. So, he arranged for one of my brothers to take me to Texas to live with him until I could find a job and move out on my own.

When I was about 22 years old, I came back to Oklahoma for vacation to meet my two brothers-in-law on a deer-hunting trip in the Kiamichi Mountains in southern Oklahoma.

They had the camp set up, and my sisters kept the coffee boiling all day because it was cold. Since I didn't know the area, I was a little reluctant to go hunting, so I gathered wood and did chores around the camp. About the third day, I thought I'd go hunting, so I figured if I went down the side of the mountain and crossed over and set up where I could see the smoke from the campfire, I would have no problem.

However, I found some big buck tracks and followed them and got lost. All day I tried to find my way back to camp. Late in the evening, I shot a squirrel with my .30-30 rifle so I would have something to eat if I was out all night. It blew the squirrel apart, and all I could keep was the two back legs.

Just before dark, I came across a dirt road, so I thought I'd stay on it in case the guys came around looking for me. I walked down the road until I came to a low–water bridge that I thought looked like the one I'd crossed coming into camp the first time. I turned around and walked back the other way. After about two miles, I heard someone chopping wood, and I smelled smoke, so I thought I'd ask them for directions. I knew we were camped on Sawmill Road, so I hoped they would take me there if I was far from their camp.

It was pretty dark, so I was careful how I approached the camp, but it just so happened to be our camp. Of course, the women were worried, but the men told them I'd grown up in the woods and knew how to find my way home. They planned to drive around the next morning to look for me.

My brother-in-law Billy said when I got hungry, I'd show up. My sister Virgie said I used to hunt as a kid and always came home just at supper time. My brother-in-law Doyle said he was going to eat, since the venison stew was ready.

I stepped out into the light and said I was just waiting for it to get ready. I showed them the two squirrel legs and told them I brought

some meat for the pot. They sure got a kick out of that.

It was many years later at a family reunion that I told them the truth.

My Fishing Trip with Doyle Walls

by Richard Metcalf

One year when I was a teenager, my brother-in-law, Doyle Walls, invited me to go on a vacation with him to do some fishing.

I was all excited because I knew it would be a lot of fun. Doyle had an old pickup that he fixed up with a piece of plywood to make an upper section for sleeping. He slept on the bed of the pickup, and I climbed up on the top section.

It was almost dark when we got to the place we had picked out, so we unloaded everything and decided to go to bed.

I didn't sleep very well since I was excited, and early the next morning, I was ready to get up. But I accidentally dropped a metal chair and hit him in the head. He got up hollering and fussing, and I think he was about ready to take me home right then, but he calmed down finally.

That evening when we went fishing, we caught a good

mess of catfish, so I tied them off to a root of a tree while we finished getting set up to cook.

When we were ready, he told me to go get the fish so we could clean them. It was beginning to get dark by then, so we knew we would have to hurry to get everything done.

When I went to get the fish, they were gone. The root I tied them to wasn't secured. It was just stuck in the ground and looked okay. The fish had pulled it loose and gotten free. Even though they were on a stringer, we couldn't find them.

After Doyle finished his cussing and fussing, he decided we would go on home that night.

He never invited me to go on a vacation again.

Honorable Mention

Valentine's Day Poetry Contest

Many Times

by Richard Metcalf

Many times, we wait too long
To say what should be said.
I want to say I'm glad you came along
To share my life and what's ahead.
I love you.
Happy Valentine Day

Progress

by Richard Medcalf

On a frosty November morning
Just about dawn,
I saw the ducks take wing.

I watched them slowly disappear
With grace and beauty.
As they glided along,
I heard morning singing.

Songs of nature,
Such wondrous sounds.
Tunes that leave you humming,
Memories swirling round and round.

Times of youth and freedom,
Fishing, hunting, camping and friends.

Looking back at childhood
Makes me wonder why it has to end.

But years pass and time sends changes.
Progress, they tell us.
They dam up all the rivers,
Tear down all the forest.
Supposed to be better for us.

When I think of flying squirrels and rabbits,
I don't see how that can be.
I think they are messing up the world.
What they call progress is destruction to me.

Robert's Ghost Dance

By Richard Medcalf

Last week, my brother Robert and his wife Silvia came to visit. We sat around the table playing a card game called Phase 10. It was raining outside, and a storm was blowing in, so my wife Wanda suggested they stay the night with us. Later that evening, we ate a snack and continued our card game while the wind was howling. It was getting dark early.

There was a loud thump on the wall outside, and Wanda said, "What was that?"

I told her not to worry. It was just the wind blowing some things against the outside wall.

It wasn't very long until there was another thump, and Wanda just about fell off her chair. We all laughed at her, and I told her it was the bogey-man wanting in out of the weather.

She didn't like that much, so she said, "Go see what it

is. Someone might be needing help."

Robert said he would go check it out. I told him not to bother. It was raining hard and was so dark you couldn't see three feet in front of your face.

Wanda said, "Please go check it out."

Well, anyone who has been married knows when a woman says, "Please," she really means get off your behind and go do it.

Robert put on his coat and cap and went to the door. Sure enough, it was so bad he couldn't see much at all. Just as he stepped off the porch, a gust of wind blew a piece of plastic that hit him in the face and wrapped itself around his arms and shoulders, so he thought for sure a monster had him. He started kicking and jumping and yelling as we watched through the screen door. We busted out laughing so hard we had tears rolling down our faces while he fought that plastic.

Finally, he turned the right way, and the wind blew the plastic away. He saw us laughing at him and was mad at first, but he walked over to us and said, "I'm glad that was just a baby monster. I sure wouldn't want to tangle with the parents." And we all started laughing even harder.

All during the night as we stayed up and played cards, Robert and his "Ghost Dance."

Special Angel

by Richard Medcalf

The Lord said to Vergie,
"You've got a mountain to climb.
But I'll be here to help you
When it comes your time."

"When you're halfway up
And find it hard to climb,
I'll give you a pair of angel wings
To help you get by."

"When you reach the top of the mountain,
I'll open those golden gates wide
To welcome my special Angel,
So you, Vergie, can sit here by My side."

Speculation

by Richard Medcalf

Look! There an eagle soars
Up in the clear blue sky
Above the haze of smog and stink
Created by mankind.

Once his world was beauty,
Rabbits and squirrels and food aplenty.
But change has come with population,
So-called civilization.

Once he lived as king on high,
But time has passed him by.
Like the Indians of yesterday,
Legends of old have passed away.

Civilization brings us change.
Sometimes better, often worse.
But life goes on, and all things
Sooner or later return to dust.

The Funeral

by Richard Medcalf

There comes time in all our lives,
When we lose a loved one.
These times are always painful,
But life must still go on.

We all go back together
To help each other through the sorrow.
It's hard to get a good night's sleep,
But we have a lot to face tomorrow.

When it comes time to face the task
of sitting through the ceremony,
You need to have someone to lean on
to keep from feeling lonely.

When you have the burial,
And you're lowering the casket of a close friend,
You can feel your heartstrings clutching.
It seems so final, like the end.

But there should be a sense of peace,
Even though his life is over.
We need to rejoice and be happy for him,
For the funeral is really the gateway to heaven.

The Marine

by Richard Medcalf

All the people gathered around.
They had heard the news
That had been spread around.
One of the town's favorite sons
Would finally be coming home.

Soon the bus was in sight.
Family members had tears in their eyes.
The bus stopped, and the doors opened wide.
The driver got up and helped him outside.

He came back home with only one leg.
The other, he left behind.
He smiled real big and hollered real loud,
"Hallelujah, Mom I'm home!"

They all gathered around him with hugs,
Holding him tight and shaking his hand.
The whole town was showing him love,
Knowing the Marines had made him a man.

The Race

by Richard Medcalf

Their horses were running
Across the wide plains.
They were racing the weather
To beat the lightning and rain.

She was on a mustang.
He was on a paint.
Hell-bent-for-leather,
As homeward they came.

The mustang was faster,
Surefooted and fleet.
She dug in her spurs,
Her darling to beat.

As he topped the hill,
He saw the mustang was down
And the body of Sheila
Lying there on the ground.

His heart started pounding
As he ran to her side.
For he knew at a glance,
His darling had died.

Large salty tears fell like the rain.
Never in his life had he known such pain.
He'd be alone now for the rest of his life,
With nothing but loneliness, heartache, and strife.

For a man with no woman
Is only existing,
With no reason to live,
No will for resisting.

Writer's Dilemma

by Richard Medcalf

I'm working twelve hours a day,
Seven days a week.
Now that I'm over fifty,
I need more beauty sleep.

So, I set my alarm for six o'clock,
And I go to bed early at night.
With that much rest,
I should be able to make it all right.

But it never fails.
On a night when I know I have a hard day ahead,
I can't go to sleep.
These lines of rhyme tumble through my head.

So I get me a pad and pen,
Turn on the light by my bed.
Now that I'm ready to write,
My mind goes blank,
And I fall asleep instead.

Photo provided by author

ABOUT AUSTIN MIDDLEBROOK

Austin Middlebrook entered Ada Writer's Valentine's Day Poetry Contest and won third place! He lives in Atoka, Oklahoma.

3rd Place Winner

Valentine's Day Poetry Contest

Eternity

by Austin Middlebrook

When I was young,
my Father told me,
"Son, forgive your enemies
so you will not depart from me.

Though this world holds riches
and enticing things,
do not be led astray
for I am He who saves.

I love you son.
Have faith in me.
I'll descend one day
to take you to eternity."

ABOUT DON PERRY

Don Perry grew up near Crockett, Texas and later moved to Fort Worth. He joined the Marines and served his final duty station at MCAAS Yuma, where he met the love of his life, Barbara. They had two children and three grandchildren.

After many years in the aviation field he retired and moved to Ada, Oklahoma. He now writes poetry and short stories of his youth and life's experiences. He wrote a fictional book in the modern western genre, "Little Texas on the Pecos". Currently he has two novels 'in the works'. All 'Round Cowboy is a sequel to Little Texas on the Pecos and 'The Wereric' is written in science fiction genre.

Anna Lee

By Don Perry

I signed aboard that old ship Anna Lee,
Surprised they even considered me.
A lad of twelve with no history of the sea
and no thought of what was to ever be.

The first mate was a scurvied old man
With a toothless grin and weathered hands.
He was deathly gaunt and truly tan,
With a sad look to far-off lands.

At high tide, she cast her lines before!
The lines to aft were no more!
The mainsail set for a distant shore,
With anchor drawn and chains in store.

It was first time I did thirst
For my home and solid earth.
The ocean blew in furrows deep.
My evening meal I could not keep.

The boson smiled as the bow plunged deep.
The captain gave me his bunk to sleep.
My only chore the deck to sweep,
I ventured out from my protected keep.

The waves did split fast and free.
Three sheets of sail in front of me,
I felt her lurch, then turn to the lea.
Swift was the soul of Anna Lee.

The wind in my face forever blew.
‘Twas the first time I ever knew
The call to be upon the windy sea
Aboard that swift ship, Anna Lee.

Now, as captain upon that billowed sea,
With fathoms to flow beneath my feet,

A windy gale now blows over me,
And fills a set of trusted sheets.

Plunge the bow deep into that frothy wave.
Hold the tiller true, and trim the foresail fast,
Let me stand upon the deck, true and brave
And catch a glimpse of my youthful home, at last

I Buried Old Blue Today

By Don Perry

I buried Blue today with sadness in my heart.
He had a good stop and a willing start.
His gait was soft as a velvet cloth.
With a watchful eye, his judgment never off.

Years took their toll. On me too, I guess.
We were partners. We were friends, no less.
We rode the high country at the start.
On a snow-covered ridge, he won my heart.

I'm retired now, and so was he.
Through thick and thin, he never gave up on me.
He took me there and brought me back
My love for him did never lack.

His heart gave out without a doubt.
With arthritis and colic had he many a bout.
I found him while going to give him hay.
He would have been thirty-four, come this May

We'll ride on heaven's green grass someday,
Young once more, we'll run and play.
I dug deep and laid him gently on a bed of hay.
With a broken heart, I buried old Blue today.

The Real Story

by Don Perry

Jedidiah Wilkins was smart, you could tell. At a young age he already knew his numbers and could read the Bible good as any nine-year-old. Knew some verses too. He had an ornery streak in him as well. His pa always said, “That there Jedidiah, he’s going to be somebody, maybe even get into politics. You just wait ‘n’ see.”

His ma named him Jedidiah because it meant “Loved by God” and she figured he was so pretty a baby that God surely must love him. She was wrong.

Jed was just a little sharper than most people and that, coupled with being ornery, made him dangerous. He once backed his mule into a city feller that was bent over looking for a moonshine still. That mule planted both hooves right in the seat of that revenuer’s pants. Knocked him clean off that road into the holler below.

By the time he turned ten years old, Jed accidentally led

a chicken home with corn kernels and tenacity. He led that chicken all the way across the road and into the hay barn. His pa didn't cotton to stealing outright, but if Jeb could convince a chicken to find a new home, it was just fine with him. The only thing was that the chicken was a cockerel. Not much good for anything but wringing his neck and frying him up early. Every morning that little rooster would climb up on the hay bales and crow at the first crack of dawn, waking everyone up with its unceasing crowing. It would even crow just before sunset. The thing the little rooster did best was crow.

Finally, Jed's pa took him aside, "Look here, son, you got to do something about that chicken. Your Ma, she likes to sleep in sometimes. Where'd you get that bird anyhow?"

"Well, Pa, I ain't gonna lie. I stole him from across the road. They got too many roosters, and they ain't gonna miss him."

"Your Ma ain't gonna miss him either if he wakes her up just one more time, if you know what I mean." His pa winked and made a firing pistol sign with his hand. "I'll tell you what. You go put him back across the road, and everything will just be all right."

Jed gathered the bird up and headed across the road. He hid in the bushes by the old wagon until he sensed the coast was clear, then creeped across the yard in his best sneaking up form. Just as he was about to reach for the door of the hen house, Preacher Jones poked his head out and said, “Boy! I said boy! What cha’ doing there? You stealin’ the chickens, are ya?”

Jed leaped about six feet straight up and tried to get his heart back into his chest. “What? I aint no chicken thief. I was just putting this here rooster back ‘cause he crows and wakes up my ma every morning. Honest injun.”

“You expect me to believe that you’re putting a chicken back? Hog wash! Haven’t you ever been taught ‘Thou shalt not steal’? That’s number eight on the list.”

The deacon took the bird from Jed and motioned back toward the road. “You’re Clem Wilkins boy, ain’t you? What’s your name, boy?”

“I’m Jedidiah Wilkins. I just wanted to put the rooster back, so my ma won’t shoot him. Honest, that’s all.”

“Well, you might ought to git on back home. I suppose you and yours might as well come down to the church on Sunday. Git some Bible in you.” He held the little rooster a little higher and looked at it. “Sherriff Tate don’t cotton to chicken thieves. You know what I mean?”

Jed glanced around toward the road, “Yes, sir, I reckon I know what you mean”

Jed walked back across the road and spotted his father waiting for him. “How’d it go? You git that little bird back?”

“Yessir, but the preacher caught me, accused me of stealing chickens. He said we got to come down to church come Sunday.”

“That’s too bad. I reckon that preacher’s going to ruin your good name, spreading it around that you’re a chicken thief.”

“I didn’t steal any chicken, Pa!”

It’s about time we get you a new start and all. Maybe change your name, too. Your Aunt Clinton, down at Hope, Arkansas, she’ll put you up. And we can call you William. Besides, you ain’t never going to make it in politics if you can’t even steal a proper chicken.”

“But, Pa! Let me repeat! I did not steal that chicken!

Writer's Dreams

by Don Perry

If I could but capture the stories of my dreams,
But as I wake, they come apart at the seams.
There is this story there of some great magnitude,
Of murder and mayhem in vivid scenes

They taunt and tease me like wisps of smoke,
Only to vanish in the morning light, as if some joke.
Their essence within confounds me but remains.
The puzzle does not fade. My interest they provoke.

These dreams could produce a story or a book,
Welcome within my mind. Take a good look.
For it is the place the story does remain
Within my subconscious in some hidden nook.

ABOUT JULIANNA PETITE

Julianna wrote songs, poetry, and short stories long before she self-published her first book in 2016. In high school, her peers called her Julius since she played lead guitar in an all-girls' band, the BackGears, singing first soprano and harmony to her own melodies and to the music of other popular groups like the Beatles. At the time, most girls simply watched the boys.

Upon high school graduation, she desired to remain in Oklahoma near her family, choosing the field of education at the university. She considered this choice gave her security and safety, not foreseeing where her future choices might pluck her out of Oklahoma and land her on the other side of the world. It did, but not to worry, she came back home.

In the only two writing contests she entered for short stories, she won first place in both. She attends workshops with published writers such as Mel Odom and Merline Lovelace—action-adventure-romance writers. She is a member of several writers' groups, Oklahoma Writers' Federation, Inc. and the Writing for Fun group meeting weekly on Tuesday, at Pontotoc Technology Center, Ada, Oklahoma.

Find Julianna's books at her website

https://www.juliannapetite.com

America's Future ~ Global Agenda

or go to **Amazon.**

Check out her published novels in the Dimension series:

Red Dirt Road
Down Mexico Way

You can find her books listed above at Amazon or more easily from her website where you might read a few chapters to see if you enjoy the rest of the adventure. Third in her Dimension series is the upcoming novel *Salt Creek* published in a short introductory excerpt for this Creations 2020 publication

1st Place Winner

Short Story Contest

Angie's Choice

by Julianna Petite

Angie grimaced as she lay flat on what she knew must be a doctor's uncomfortable examination table. However, she wondered how she got here. She felt no physical pain. She had long blocked emotional grief.

Why can't I remember why I came?

She glanced at the full-length mirror. Whoever planned this doctor's office possessed no sensitivity. As a skilled decorator . . .

Skilled decorator? Am I a decorator?

Whoever Angie was, she knew she would eliminate the mirror for the patient's sake. No reflections of sickly faces in an examination room seemed appropriate.

She continued to frown at her reflection.

Angie, when did you get so old? She turned away, troubled.

On the opposite wall hung a homey display in sharp contrast to other sterile corners.

Family portraits?

Angie knew her own skilled technique in any home interior decoration would have placed each masterpiece in the same arrangement. It looked homespun. And in the center of all the photos sat the largest framed portrait of a handsome man with a beautiful woman holding three smiling children bursting with laughter.

Joy. Angie's choices led her to miss that feeling.

Each additional picture hung in sequence from small children to teens. She could not criticize the artful placement. She would have arranged them the same.

An abrupt tap on the door moved Angie's eyes to the entrance where a man, garbed in white lab jacket over navy blue slacks with a light-blue dress shirt, rushed in. He kept looking at his wristwatch.

“You’re the man in the pictures.” Angie pointed. "Beautiful children.”

He finally looked up. “Mom arranges that.” He shrugged. “Home decorator.” His startling blue eyes matched the unusual shade of Angie’s grandfather’s. He smiled. “I’m Dr. Samuels.”

“Samuels? That’s my name.”

He stepped closer. “Do you know why you’re here?”

“I’m certain you’ll tell me.” She breathed.

“The test came back positive.”

“Positive?”

“Breast cancer.”

Angie nodded, confused. “Haven’t they found the cause for breast cancer, yet?”

The doctor shook his head and shrugged again. “One study cites women who choose abortion have about a fifty percent higher rate of breast cancer than those who choose life.”

She frowned. “I’m certain they’re depressed too, a woman killing her baby. I wish information had been available when I was a girl. I had an abortion. I wish a lot of things.” She stopped spilling troubles. She never conceived after her choice. “You’re very tall, Doctor, like my dad.”

He nodded. “Call me Sam.”

***

Startled awake, Angie's eyes jerked open. She lay on her self-reupholstered couch at Fourteenth Street. Her waitress job paid for the cheap room, but her decorating talents made it cozy. The baby kicked.

Scheduled for an abortion today, she walked to the mirror and felt relieved as she looked nothing like the old woman in her troubled dream.

She looked at her protruding belly and spoke to him. "OK. I'll call you Sam."

Coming Soon from Julianna Petite

-Salt Creek-

When Fox Jeffery comes home from the Middle East, he's delayed in Washington, D.C., to brief elected officials, bureaucrats, and even enemy political leaders of the men he fought in Afghani air-space. When he finally heads for Oklahoma, Fox wonders if his background as a combat fighter pilot is up to playing tentative investigator into questions waiting for him as he travels. When Ruby Marsh, his secretary, unexpectedly joins the search for answers, he wonders if their investigation into the long robes, missing women, and political intrigue will find a solution, or will the threat turn back on them?

Excerpt from Salt Creek

Opal started to set the table, but she paused with the dishes in her grip as she looked outside and saw the old milk cow standing under the cool shade of an oak tree. She yelled to her husband. “It looks like Greentree’s going to have twins again, Frank.”

Instead of commenting, Frank frowned as he approached from the living room. He paused in the doorway. “He won’t be coming home.”

Opal’s attention swung back to her small, cozy kitchen. She hurriedly placed the dishes on the table and then grabbed her heart. Her hands trembled as she turned back to look at her husband. “What did you say?”

“He’s not coming.”

She held onto the table as she released a low moan. “They’ve killed him!”

The old man sucked in a heavy breath as he hurried to comfort her. “No, Opal. That’s not what I said.”

“But he’s due home. What happened this time? Did he call?”

Frank nodded as he embraced her.

The woman grimaced. “He didn’t ask to talk to me?”

He shook his head. “He said he didn’t have time to explain. He’d tell us when he knew he could come.”

“He doesn’t even know why he can’t come home after another year? They’ve had him over there almost three years.”

"He's not in the Middle East right now."

"He's here?"

"In Washington."

"And they won't let him come home?"

"He'll be here, soon. Don't be so upset. Maybe next week. You said yesterday you didn't have the groceries you wanted. You'll have plenty of time to shop now."

"I can always shop. I want my son home."

"He's in the military! You can't expect him to respond to Mama every time you want him home."

"I do expect him to ask to speak to his mother instead of only talk to his father. That's what I expect."

The man released his gentle hold on her and started walking away. "Opal, he's almost thirty-five now, isn't he? You're going to have to get used to it. I have after all this time. We can't expect him to come home at our beck and call. Especially now, when the national security of our nation might be at stake."

"National security of our nation!" She grumbled under her breath. "What does national security care about my son? It's already got him shot up more than once. They even reported him dead."

"But he wasn't. And he escaped. So, hold your horses and wait."

The woman released a heavy breath. “Easy for you to say. You got to talk to him.” She pinched a bite off the casserole. “Not enough salt.” She talked to herself and added more.

“You were out tending those daisies when he

called . . ..”

“Roses, thank you! And you could have told him he couldn’t hang up until he spoke to me.”

“He hung up on me, too. I started asking questions, and he just said he had to go. He rushed to tell me he wouldn’t be here this week. He said he couldn’t come, he had briefings. Then he would probably be here next week.”

“Probably? I thought you said he would definitely be here next week—not probably.”

“Yes. But now I’m trying to remember exactly what he said. Next time I won’t answer the phone at all.”

“Now that’s hateful.”

“No, that’s just staying safe to make sure that any questions you have will either be answered correctly, or we’ll just stay in the dark.”

“Frank Jeffery! You would do that, wouldn’t you?”

“You betcha. I don’t like answering for my son when I barely got to talk with him myself. And now I’m being needled by his Mama.”

"Needled! You call my concern for my only son, needling?" The elderly woman shook her head. "We'd better be seeing him next week, or I might just make a trip to Washington, D.C., to see what's the matter."

Frank sat down in his chair and sipped the sweet tea Opal brought him. He nodded. "If you're so all fired up to see where he is, that's fine with me. I'll wait 'til he comes home. I've better things to do."

"Better things like sitting in your easy chair? No, I won't allow it! If I go, you go. This is our only son, Frank Jeffery! You haven't seen him in three years. And now it looks like you're barely going to see him this year. You're going to take me to Washington if he's not coming home."

"Uh-uh." He shook his head and sat back to reach for the remote. "No, I'm not." He took another gulp of tea.

"We're going, I tell you. We're going, if he's not here by next week."

"Who would work with him? I tell you, he's rude." Ruby Marsh wrinkled her nose and shook her head.

"Ruby, who cares how rude that man is?" Emma James sighed in exaggeration, licking her lips. "He's a dream."

"A what?" Ruby couldn't believe Emma referred to Major Fox J. Jeffery as a dream. "You are a married woman!"

"Yeah, I know. Ain't that a shame?" Emma smiled

wickedly.

"He's a nightmare." Ruby lifted her hands pointing left and right mimicking him. "Get me this. Bring me that. You haven't found it? You'd better look. You'll have to work overtime!" Ruby shook her head again. "No I'm not going to work overtime. I am going home next week. Thank you!"

Emma giggled. "I would love to work overtime with him."

Ruby sighed in exasperation. "I'm going to tell your husband."

"Hmm." Emma nodded. "I might tell him myself."

Ruby lifted her palms up. "Then trade me bosses. I've only been assigned to him one week—one week! It feels like a whole year as much as I've jumped around doing what he's asked. Saturday, I'm headed for Oklahoma on vacation—a much-needed vacation—after two years here. And now I get assigned Major Jeffery for a boss? You're going to have to look for a different secretary, Emma. He's always asking me to do six things when I'm not finished with the seven, he just gave me."

Emma turned to the Major's door, stretching her arms wide as she cooed, "Oh, ask me Major, just ask me . . . anything."

"Stop it!" Ruby stridently whispered. "He'll hear you."

"Well, he'll hear you complaining, too."

"Listen Emma, I've got to type this!" She lifted what looked to be a ream of paper. "This . . . monster . . . is at least two-hundred pages of his hand-written notes—HAND WRITTEN NOTES! And it's due by tomorrow. He just handed it to me. Hopefully I can make out the words."

"Oh, that's easy. You've got a word processor."

"Hmm. Easy for you Miss Emma, with speed typing expertise—and your mastery in reading barbed-wire for words. Now, scoot out so I can operate here."

The Major's door opened. He stepped out with Senator Leonard's daughter attached to his arm. "Yes ma'am. I told your father I would escort you there."

"Oh, Fox. Don't call me ma'am. That makes me sound so old."

"Sorry, old habits die hard."

"So, why can't you take me next week?"

"I've a commitment in Oklahoma."

The woman on his arm protested. "Oklahoma?"

Ruby frowned at hearing the word Oklahoma. That's where she was headed. Emma looked down at Ruby with wide eyes. She mouthed a question with no voice. "Are you traveling with the hunk to Oklahoma?"

Ruby rolled her eyes and realized too late that the major saw her facial expression. "Miss Marsh, do you have something in your eye?"

"Yes, sir." Ruby's face turned red. *It's you and your girlfriend.* She patted her eye. "There, it's gone."

The major didn't look convinced. "Have you got my notes typed?"

Ruby lowered her brow at the question. "You just handed them to me, sir."

He nodded. "An hour ago. I thought you might have some finished. Hand them to me when you have twenty pages typed so I can check it. I have to turn them in before I leave town."

Teresa questioned. "Why are you going to Oklahoma, Fox? It's so . . ."

Emma turned toward her. "It's so filled with cowboys . . . and Indians . . . the wild west. It sounds exciting. Is it Major?"

He smiled at her. "No, I don't think it's quite the wild west anymore, Mrs. James. But it's home."

Ruby frowned. "Home, sir? You mean your home?"

Teresa laughed. "Oh, I hope not!"

Fox corrected. "Mom and Dad's home. They're expecting me."

"Oh, I see." Teresa Leonard wrinkled her nose as though a foul smell drifted in the air. "I'm so glad you're escorting me to the ball tonight. And after your trip to Oklahoma, I hope to see you again."

He nodded. "Likewise. See you, tonight." He turned toward Ruby. "Miss Meadows, what time is that other meeting I'm supposed to make today?"

Ruby checked his calendar. "It's in an hour. I'll notify you thirty minutes before your gathering just like I did for the senator's powwow."

Teresa laughed. "You are calling a senators' meeting a powwow?"

Fox nodded. "I knew what she meant. I'm from Oklahoma, remember?" He turned back to his office and closed the door.

The woman kept standing there looking at the closed entrance.

Emma frowned at her back. "Miss Leonard, it looks like you've never had to deal with a busy man who closes the door in your face."

Teresa turned and eyed Emma with a scowl. "I can't believe Fox is traveling to Oklahoma."

"Me neither." Ruby shook her head, her face reflecting disapproval.

But Emma stepped in front of Ruby's line-of-sight and crossed her arms. "I make all the flight arrangements. I'll assure you he's headed for Oklahoma—if only temporarily."

Ruby heard rather than watched the woman stomp out of the room. "Why did you emphasize that, Emma? I think you made her mad."

"Who cares? She's a little spoiled flirt."

"Emma James, she's not so bad. And what are you thinking by making a senator's daughter mad?"

"It's not what I'm thinking—it's what I'm going to do. I've been watching my favorite typist these past two years, and since I'm already happily married—I have the man of my dreams—I don't need the major. But I think my little friend who works her butt off for me in the typing pool needs to find a man of her own."

"What are you talking about?"

Emma started laughing. "It's not what I'm talking about—it's *who* I'm talking about. You've just met him a week ago. He's from Oklahoma. You're from Oklahoma. Surely you have something in common."

Ruby grimaced. "Not that man." She pointed to the major's door. "Certainly not that man. Never."

Emma narrowed her eyes. "Why do you say that?"

"He's too . . ."

Emma laughed again. "I know. I know what you mean. He's too . . . hmm . . . that's it . . . especially in that uniform."

ABOUT NORA METCALFE RAY

Nora Ray started writing poetry in high school and has more recently started writing short stories. She writes about anything that catches her attention, extending from the true-life stories she grew up hearing to the totally fantastical. There are also many stories of faith. She grew-up in a small town and writes from a small-town, country point of view.

Nora was the third-place winner of the Ada Writers Valentine's Day Poetry Contest in 2019 with her poem, *His Valentine Candy Heart.* She has been published in Creations 2018 and Creations 2019. This year she published her book, *Tumbleweed Gardens.* It is a collection of poems and short stories and can be found at Amazon.com.

When she's not writing or doing research for her next book, she is helping her stepdad, Doyle Smith, get his books on the market. She enjoys reading a wide range of genres from classic works to the paranormal. While reading, she also serves as a bed for her two dogs, Jezebel (Jezzy), a Chihuahua, and Ladybug (Bug), a Pugapoo.

A Sad Eulogy

By Nora Metcalfe Ray

The day started out dark and dreary. Misty rain was coming down. It was a perfect day for a funeral. No one wanted to get out in it, but it would hide the tears of the few people who showed up. Most that came were there for the family, not because they cared about the man that had passed.

The body that lay in that coffin wasn't the most popular person, but he sure had a lot of pretend friends, people that were as shallow as he. All were fellow drug addicts. They needed each other to feed their addiction. There were a few good people that knew him and loved him before he turned to drugs and alcohol.

He had been saved as a young man. Troubles and temptation took him down a road he didn't want to be on, and he was weak. He prayed daily to be delivered from temptation, but it wasn't meant to be.

The man in the coffin wasn't old by today's standards. Drugs and fast living had cut his life short. It made him look ninety years old. He had stooped shoulders and snow-white hair, although he wasn't sixty yet.

His eulogy wouldn't take long to tell; it was simple enough. His parents were dead, and his kids didn't care enough to show up. His sisters only wanted to appear to care. They wanted him cremated so there would be no need for a service. They didn't want to spoil the holidays.

You see, Thanksgiving was more important than their brother. He was such an embarrassment, a bother. They told none of his friends he had passed. They weren't welcome. They made the family look bad, because they truly cared. It wasn't even put in the paper. The people who really cared didn't have a chance to say good-bye or bring flowers for a gentle soul that was so confused and misunderstood. He died alone at home without anyone to hold his hand or shed a tear.

So you see, the rain is good. His family won't have to pretend to cry, because nature will provide the false evidence. And Heaven will cry for the sad soul of one of their lost brothers.

He now rests in Heaven with the Father and Brother that loved him best. The Brother that died to save him and the Father that loved him before he was ever born.

A Wanted Man

by Nora Metcalfe Ray

We all saw him ride in on that big black stud.
He looked mad as hell as he tread in the mud.
He walked in the saloon and laid his money down.
He acted like he owned this little shanty town.

He wore his Stetson low to cover his eyes.
It was plainly clear he wasn't here to socialize.
He heard the click as she pulled the hammer back.
He whipped around, eyes flashing like a maniac.

In a soft voice she said, "You're a wanted man."
He knew her at once. She was Marianne.
She lived across the valley when they were young.
He had a black horse, but she always rode a dun.

“What’s the meaning of this?” I heard him say.
“You done me wrong. Now you’re gonna pay,”
She said with a smile on her pretty tan face,
Standing there in petticoats, gingham, frills, and lace.

“I’ve broke no laws. I’m not wanted anywhere,”
I heard him say as he just stood there.
“That’s where you’re wrong. It’s simple to see.”
Then she said, “You’re wanted by me.”

Aunt Gerty

by Nora Metcalfe Ray

There it is, my second home. The first time I came to visit was back in 1972. I had just graduated from grade school. Granny thought it was about time I met some of her family. We loaded up that old `59 Ford truck and headed to the boondocks. Aunt Gerty was my Granny's favorite sister. Gertrude Estella, was her proper name, but we all just called her Gerty.

Gerty was 4'11" of rompin', stompin', toothless sass! What we call a crusty old broad down here. She wore long, bohemian-style dresses with Army boots. She was born in a tent on a creek bed and was the youngest of ten kids. She always said, "I'm a scrapper from a way back!"

I never knew exactly how old she was, but she looked ancient to that 12-year-old. Sunbaked, golden skin covered her tiny bone structure. Her hair was white as snow, illuminating ice-blue eyes that danced with mischief.

Now I've grown up since then and have a family of my own. But I still adore Aunt Gerty. I haven't been back here in years. Since the government shut my job down and ordered our churches closed, I thought now would be as good a time as any to come visit.

"Coronavirus! Huh, I remember Uncle Herbie having that Coronavirus. He drank a case of Corona beer a day until it finally killed him at the young age of 102! But it never gave him the runs, so why are them crazy city fellers hoarding toilet paper?" Aunt Gerty asked.

"When we were kids, if we didn't have any toilet paper handy, we just used what we had—newspaper, old catalogs, leaves. But if you go with them leaves, you better watch out for that there poison ivy! That'll sure make life interesting fer ya. Your ole hiney might be a itchin' and a oozin' for a month of Sundays if you make that mistake! Won't be able to sit down neither," smirked Aunt Gerty, as she spit a trail of tobacco (pronounced ta-back-ey) across the yard.

"Now we always had plenty of wash cloths; they are washable and reusable! Just like cloth diapers. It's a waste to hoard plastic diapers in times like these! Smear a little Vaseline, slap on a cloth diaper, and there you go! They's all washable," said Aunt Gerty.

<><><><><>

Red Eye Junction is the closest town to Aunt Gerty's place. Its 216 residents are what Aunt Gerty calls "them big city fellers."

Shortly after I got here, Aunt Gerty went to pay her bills. I rode along just for company. Now, I'm not sure that was such a good idea.

"Where we going, Aunt Gerty?" I asked.

"Gotta pay my bills," she said.

"Why not just mail them in?" I asked.

"Nope, been doin' it this way for the last forty years or more," she said. "Look at that! They's closed! They ain't never closed before. What's that sign on the door say?"

"I'll go look," I said. After walking up to the door, I realized she wasn't gonna like this. "Uh, Aunt Gerty, they closed for the Coronavirus. They don't want to get sick. It says to mail in your payment."

"They just usin' that as an excuse. They want me to have to pay extry for the postage. Well, I ain't a gonna do it!" Gerty ranted, spitting a stream of tobacco. "I've been paying my bills this way for forty plus years. I've been out in the middle of my 240 acres. I ain't contaminated! Crazy city fellers!"

"Now calm down. It's for your protection, too." I said.

"No, it ain't. They just crazy city slickers! This is the land of stupid. Stupid, stupid, stupid. That's all there is to it. They's gonna collapse the economy, closing everything down. Look at that. Not a car in sight! They want me to mail my bills, but the Post Office is closed. What's their sign say?" Gerty fumed.

I got out and read the sign, "They have changed their hours of operation." I said.

"Well, that's just great. Now I can't even get my mail!" said Aunt Gerty, turning red in the face. She stomped on the accelerator and floored it all the ten miles back to her house.

I was afraid to ask her what she planned to do. I could almost see the steam coming out her ears.

"I been thinkin'," said Aunt Gerty.

Oh no, here it comes, I thought.

"They are just scaremongers! Trying to price gouge the customers, with that 50-cent postage stamp. If you lick the envelope to seal it, you are sending your saliva through the mail, so that means you are sending your germs! Isn't that called terrorism, sending a potential threat through the US mail? What makes that any safer than going in?" Aunt Gerty wanted to know. "They can just kiss my bloomers!"

Well, it took a couple of days, but Aunt Gerty started to settle down, just about the time we found a corpse in the back yard.

Early Morning Coffee Blues

By Nora Metcalfe Ray

I wake way too early.
I've barely been asleep.
One eye slowly opens,
As I surface from the deep

I try to doze back off,
But I know it is no use.
My brain has started rambling.
It's sleep deprivation abuse.

I finally roll out of bed
And stumble to the kitchen
To get the coffee on.
My early-morning addiction.

My brain starts to function
As my coffee starts to perk.
What is it about this bean
That makes my brain work?

I'm finally ready to face the day.
It's too late to go back and snooze.
Tomorrow will start it all over again,
My Early Morning Coffee Blues

Old Age

By Nora Ray

I got me some old-age flab
On these old-age abs.
Piled on my old-age back
And my sac-a-rilly-ac.

Give me some old-age meds
And some old-age pads
Mixed with some old-age lotion.
That's quite a potion!

These old-age shoes
Really give me the blues.
And this old-age gray hair
I dye black with a flair!

This getting old ain't no fun.
It sure ain't for the young,
`Cause my false teeth no longer fit,
And it's even hard to sit and sh*t!

So, give me some coffee
And some cinnamon toffee.
Then I can face my last days
In this old foggy haze.

To the nursing home I'll go.
Probably put on quite a show.
Cause senile I'll be.
Guess I'll just sit and drink tea!

Children of the South

By Nora Metcalfe Ray

Yes, we are children of the South. We don't think like you do. We been raised on grits, collard greens, biscuits and fried chicken. No, not the Colonel's. We bread ours at home. We wear our hearts on our sleeve and bless a lot of hearts! But we're tough as nails when we have to be. This is the South. We ain't got no back-up in us. We fight for what we believe in.

We're taught grace as a way of life. Stand on your own two feet. God is real. America is worth fighting for. Lend your neighbor a hand. Give him a hand up, NOT a handout!

Your logic isn't always our logic. You see logic only through your scientific brain. Our logic comes through our upbringing, Bible, and heart. What you see as gray areas, we see only black and white. You've heard it said, "God said it, we believe it, and that settles it!" But I say, it doesn't matter if we *believe* it. God said it, and that settles it!

Many cultures and religions have invaded the South since the Confederate States tried to secede from the nation. A lot of people living here now think like Yankees. But we still have strong Southern values here in the Confederate States.

I'm not talking slavery. This is not a black and white issue. It's a people issue. It's simply a way of thinking. I have many black friends that think like I do. We want America back. We want our Constitution back. We want our Bill of Rights, and we want the government OUT of our business.

ABOUT ANITA BLACKWELL ROBERTSON

Earning a degree in Performing Arts and English, Anita

did nothing with either of those until later in life. Instead, she became a professional calligrapher. Her company, The Scribe and Scroll, became the family business with her husband and children framing her artwork. They traveled around the United States for 15 years doing art shows as well as selling her pieces to stores.

She dabbled in poetry and wrote some of the pieces she completed in calligraphy, but she did not pursue writing until early 2019 when she joined the weekly Writing for Fun group. Through the encouragement of others in the group, she took classes, read books on how to write, became a member of the Jerry Jenkins Writers' Guild, and started putting pen to paper—rather keyboard to screen.

She and her husband Al plan to move to the country of Jordan before the end of 2020 if international travel bans are lifted. They started a blog on their website www.refugeinjordan through which they post information about the country every other Thursday.

She recently completed a big item on her bucket list: her 93,000-word memoir *Journey to Jordan*.

2nd Place Winner

Short Story Contest

God Patrols the Badlands

by Anita Blackwell Robertson

For fifteen years, our family livelihood derived from art shows all over the U.S. I created the art, and my husband and children—Al, Alisa, and Aaron—framed it.

On July 4, 1989, we finished a show in Rapid City, South Dakota, in the southwest corner of the state. We tore down the booth and packed everything into our over-sized cargo van and five-by-eight-foot enclosed trailer. Shortly before nine o'clock, we hit I-90 heading east across the isolated Badlands. Normally, Al does not drive after sundown because the road rhythm and nightfall lull him to sleep. But thinking we would soon find a motel, he slid behind the wheel.

No vacancies anywhere in the next hamlet … or the next … or the next meant a straight-through drive. I didn't trust him to stay awake, so I determined to drive until daybreak. Lasting until five-thirty, I heard him stirring and I asked, "Can you drive an hour so I can catch a few winks? I'll take it from there."

"I think so." He sounded alert, so I felt safe handing over driving duty. "Alisa, keep an eye on your dad for me, OK?" She nodded from the passenger seat.

We previously suspended a full-size inflatable mattress behind the seats under which we stowed boxes of inventory. Al's tight-fit, engineered packing of the van and trailer was perfection.

I lay down beside Aaron and conked out. But about six o'clock, I jerked awake, my face hitting the ceiling to the sound of creaking metal.

"Did you go to sleep?"

"Yes," Al replied tersely, wrangling the steering wheel. We swerved off the highway down the deeply-recessed median, dragging the trailer behind us. Ahead was a crossover road he leaped over like a bronc rider, taking out a sign mounted on a four-by-four-inch wooden post. He plunged down the other side, still in the median. The van veered left, and he maneuvered it up onto the opposite side of the road going the wrong way. Finding a shallow place farther down, he crossed back to our side of the Interstate and pulled onto the shoulder.

Taking a deep breath, he got out to assess the damage. Only one casualty: a flat tire on the trailer. Not a piece of merchandise or display lost. No early-morning traffic meant he could change the tire right there.

The adrenalin rush dispelled any thought of sleep, so we took off and drove twelve hours straight through to our home in Tulsa.

***

Less than an hour after we pulled into our driveway, Mom called. After a few pleasantries, she asked, "Where were you at six o'clock this morning?"

"Why do you want to know?"

"Because I dreamed I saw your face screaming in terror. I woke up and fell to the floor in urgent prayer. Just wondered what I was praying for."

I thanked God silently and said, "We were in the Badlands of South Dakota trying to avoid having a fatal accident. Thanks for your help."

God Waits

by Anita Blackwell Robertson

When God wants something great done in this world,
He doesn't dispatch a legion of avenging angels,

Neither does He call forth a whirlwind
Nor ignite the fuse of volcanic fireworks.

No commandeering of troops into battle
Nor discharging zealous crusaders to holy causes.

He does not orchestrate the burst and boom of thunder
Nor fling His fiery arrows' majesty across the sky
To bring His purpose to pass.

When God wants something great done in this world,

He sends a baby … and then He waits.

Love is Not Just a Feeling

by Anita Blackwell Robertson

Our youthful passion would have scoffed at
The deep belonging we now feel,
The knowledge that our love is enhanced by,
But not dependent on, the fire in our bones.

Although our wedding garments no longer fit,
You are more exciting to me now
Than when we first joined hands at the altar.
We have journeyed far enough together
That even the wrinkles and silver-splashed hair are dear.

It is your essence that I love—
The person you have become as
Side by side, we battled our way through the dailies.
Illness, tragedy, and loss have transformed us
Into who we now are—warriors. . .overcomers.

Out of the churning cauldron of struggle
Has come the discovery that
Love is not just a feeling, but a decision.

Two rough stones when we married,
We have polished and burnished each other,
Emerging refined and secure in the vows we made,
Cleaving only to each other.

Our love will endure,
For better, for worse, for richer, for poorer,
In sickness and in health,
Until one of us gently lays the other
Into the arms of God.

Won't Let You Go

by Anita Blackwell Robinson

Jasper McCalip was set against his daughter's marriage. Dead set.

From reports in *The Stonewall Weekly News* and *The Ada Evening News*, he was hell-bent on stopping the wedding, even publicly stating he would commit murder, if necessary, to prevent it from taking place. "Nellie is not going to marry that Blackwell boy! Whatever it takes, I'll stop it," he blustered to anyone who would listen. His wife, Martha Matilda, objected but not *that* strenuously. She was worn out raising children.

Nellie Jane McCalip, four months past her sixteenth birthday, and Wesley Osile Blackwell, a twenty-two-year-old man called Bud by all who knew him, secretly secured a marriage license in late April. Knowing Jasper would try to stop them if they planned a church wedding, they made several attempts throughout the last month to elope.

Somehow, Daddy always found out. He kept his eye on Nellie from the time she sat down to breakfast until he turned down the oil lamps in the evening. He did everything he could—short of locking her in the cellar—to keep her and Bud apart.

"She thinks she's in love with him." He whined out the words to her mother. In those days people often married for convenience or necessity, not love. He and Martha Matilda were in that category.

Born in Tennessee, Jasper traveled to Illinois where he met his first wife Mary. Seeking adventure and a better life, they journeyed by train to Oklahoma Territory about 1870. But a hardscrabble existence and brutal winters threatened to send them back home. Then, they heard it was warmer in Texas, so they trekked south. Mary gave birth to eleven children, the last few born in Bowie, Texas, where she died. Jasper remarried within a few months.

Martha Matilda Hawkins Smith Taylor was a recent Texas widow with two girls, whose husband Joe had run up a large debt with Jasper. It seemed a perfect business-transaction solution—a widower needing a mother for his houseful of children and a widow having no income, burdened with an impossible liability. "If you'll help me raise these kids, I'll cancel the debt."

And so … they became man and wife.

They had three children together, making a total of fourteen mouths to feed plus their own. Selling their 200-acre farm in Bowie, they decided to move to the bustling town of Stonewall, Indian Territory, in the late 1800s. It was the largest town in the county. Oklahoma might become a state soon, and they wanted to be involved in something new and exciting. They built a fine house on forty acres and integrated into the community.

One night, a few years after they arrived, the post office mysteriously disappeared. It reappeared the next morning in “new” Stonewall three miles east where the railroad was coming through. Overnight, Old Stonewall became a suburb. New Stonewall assumed the name. Old Stonewall rechristened itself Frisco.

Bud’s family lived three miles west of there on a large parcel of land. They were merchants in Old Stonewall.

As the town moved, their businesses withered. Most of the residents gradually relocated to the new site. But the Blackwells were entrepreneurs. They would somehow manage to make a living another way.

The Blackwell clan had been in this part of the Chickasaw Nation since 1876, twenty-nine years at the time of this story. The two families knew each other well and had been good neighbors.

Jasper had nothing against Bud except he didn't want him for a son-in-law right now. Well, there was that incident a year ago where he was indicted for selling liquor. But he was a hard worker, came from a prominent family, and didn't get in trouble again.

Still, Nellie was his baby girl and much too young to marry. She *was* headstrong and not a little spoiled. Her austere, 67-year-old dad usually gave in to her ... but not this time. He would not let her go.

A little before three o'clock, Monday afternoon, May 22, 1905, Nellie and Bud sneaked to a clandestine spot to make their plans. They couldn't let each other go, and they didn't want to wait. Once they were married, there was nothing Jasper could do. There was no minimum-age law for marrying in the Chickasaw Nation.

Bud's uncle had a farm seven miles north of Stonewall in the opposite direction of Jasper's homestead. With the uncle's help, the couple decided to tie the knot at that secluded location. They got word to Rev. E. M. Myers to meet them there.

After they passed through town on the way to their wedding site, Jasper got wind of the plan. He figured they would go to Stonewall. Grabbing his shotgun, he called to his son, “Oscar! Let’s go.”

They hurried to town, galloping up and down Main Street, stirring up clouds of dust, and inquiring of everyone whether they had seen the couple. He reiterated his threat and waved his shotgun to back it up. Someone called out, “I think they headed north.” He turned his horse in pursuit.

About that time, Luke Blackwell, father of the groom, pulled up his steed, blocking the end of Main Street, a Winchester grasped firmly in his hand. He was prepared to defend his son’s life. Jasper whoaed his horse. Yeah, you could say there was a little tension in the air. Words flew back and forth. Maybe a little spittle.

Seeing a crowd gather, they decided to take the discussion down the street to the privacy of C. O. Scrivner’s livery. C. O., Jasper’s relative by marriage, put in his three cents’ worth, and the fathers cooled the conversation down as people on the street edged closer, their ears straining to hear. Luke and Jasper acted like adults, chewed the situation over a bit, and eventually decided to allow the kids to marry. Nellie and Bud would never let each other go. That seemed sure.

They probably didn’t ride off with their arms draped over each other’s shoulders, but the fathers trotted home to Frisco that afternoon, leaving Stonewall residents giddy with the excitement of the day. Unaware of the drama swirling in town, Bud and Nellie—my grandparents—were united in holy matrimony, against the odds and Jasper's considerable vigor.

Their descendants are much obliged they succeeded.

Oasis

by Anita Blackwell Robertson

Miss Lilly, a fiftyish black lady, lived in the neglected, low-income housing complex where I was the recently hired manager. Notes in her tenant file raved about the exceptional condition of her apartment. Not having the right to knock and ask to see inside, I waited several months to satisfy my curiosity until it was time for her yearly inspection.

When I stepped into the living room of her tiny one-bedroom apartment, I whished through a stargate to another universe. Not only was her home immaculate, it was a movie set from a glamorous 1940s film. Palm trees graced the corners of the room, a white chaise lounge nestled against one of them. African décor provided just the right touch of colorful spice. Her kitchen was magazine-worthy. The small, but luxurious, bedroom embraced a perfectly-made-up bed piled high with decorative pillows.

Even her bathroom and closet were flawless. Soft classical background music completed the ambience.

Miss Lilly cleaned other people's homes for a living. I couldn't imagine how she afforded all these fine things. As though she read my mind, she explained, "I am a professional thrift store shopper. I save my money until I find the perfect piece."

"You have obviously mastered the art of thrifting," I said admiringly. "Your taste is exquisite, but the care you shower on the place where you live shows you appreciate yourself as well. I wish I could bring your neighbors—one at a time—to see what can be done with these modest apartments."

She looked down, embarrassed. I continued bragging on her. She was the kind of woman anyone would be proud to call friend.

She looked up and said hesitantly, "I have a request to make."

"If it's in my power, you've got it."

"My knees aren't what they used to be, and I struggle climbing these stairs. When a ground-floor spot becomes available, could I move?"

I immediately thought of an apartment we were rehabbing. "I will have number 24 available within thirty days. Will that work for you?"

She beamed. "Yes'm, that will be fine."

I cleared my throat and changed the subject. "Miss Lilly, I'm going to have to evict your son Rafe from his apartment. I know he lost his job several months ago. He told me he got new employment but wouldn't get paid for thirty days. I said, 'I will work with you.' But he hasn't paid anything, and now he's lost his second job."

She looked me in the eye. "You're doing the right thing." Her lip quivered. "I don't know what happened to that boy. I raised him right, but he got into drugs and the wrong crowd. He won't listen to me. You do what you gotta do. Maybe it will knock some sense into him."

I struggled to maintain my composure. "You have a beautiful home, Miss Lilly. You're a shining example for everyone here."

Turning, I opened the door and was sucked outside back into the maelstrom of the drug-infested neighborhood.

Miss Lilly's Son Rafe

Rafe was a handsome, charismatic young man in his twenties. He dressed professionally, had short hair, and was clean-shaven. I liked him immediately when I met him, unaware of his drug involvement. He had a job and seemed to be a decent guy. Living two buildings down from his mom, he had his own life but was still under her watchful eye. She knew what was going on with him.

Other tenants told me about his involvement with known drug dealers at night in the complex. I know I overstepped my bounds, but I called him into to my office for a chat one day when he came to check his mail. The mailboxes were on the porch outside my office window. I tapped on the glass and motioned him in.

He stepped through my door with a smile on his face. I told him the rumors I'd heard and asked him if they were true. Caught off-guard, he couldn't quite lie fast enough. He had fallen into my trap.

"Rafe, I'm not your mother, but I'm going to give you some motherly advice."

"Yes ma'am," was his courteous reply.

"You're so young. You have your life ahead of you. If you do something stupid and wind up in jail, it will take you years to overcome that setback. Get out of this business right now. Make your mother—and me— proud. With your looks and intellect, you can be whatever you want to be."

He stood attentively. "Yes ma'am" was all he would say.

I tried hiking my left eyebrow which sometimes worked with my children and added, "You've got so much going for you. Don't screw up your life. It's none of my business, but

I like you and want you to succeed."

"I appreciate it, Miss Rose. I really do. Thank you for caring about me. I'll think about what you said."

Weeks went by, and he began avoiding me. I knew it was because he was so far behind on his rent. I posted the obligatory thirty-day notice on his door, and still, he didn't contact me. Finally, I had no choice but to proceed with the eviction.

I called our attorney, who notified the sheriff to serve him with papers. He was to appear at 9:00 a.m. for the eviction proceedings at the courthouse in thirty days. By this time, I was an old hand at throwing people out. Usually, I thought they got what they deserved, but I hoped Rafe would get hold of himself and straighten up. I longed for him to give me a reason to stop his expulsion.

He didn't show up at the hearing, so it was open and shut. I was in and out in five minutes. As I pulled out of the parking lot on that dreary, rainy day, I spied him getting out of someone's car. He made a mad dash for the courthouse, splashing water everywhere. No coat. No umbrella. He didn't see me. I knew it would take him a while to get back across town to the apartments. He didn't have a car, nor, did I suppose, money for the local transit bus.

I drove straight to his apartment at the back of the

apartment complex and posted the eviction notice on his door. It was almost 10:00 a.m., and he had until 5:00 to leave the premises. I couldn't treat him any better than I would anyone else, so I stuck to protocol. The backside of this row of buildings where he lived was out of sight from the rest of the complex. It was on that side where most of the dirty deeds took place—certainly the drug deals.

As I sat in my car, a woman pulled up next to me, not knowing I was the manager who posted the notice. She ran up to the door, read the paper, and began to cry—wail, actually. I don't know who she was. She appeared too old to be his girlfriend. More his mother's age. As she made a quick phone call to tell someone the news, I started the car and drove to my office in front of the complex.

When my day ended at 5:00, I made a loop around to his apartment to see what progress he had made. As friends carried out his mattress, he stood there and looked me in the eye for the first time in weeks. "I don't blame you, Miss Rose. It's my fault."

"I wish I didn't have to do this, Rafe. I really do. Please take good care of yourself." I wanted to hug him, but once again, I knew I couldn't show weakness. I had to be the one in charge. Everyone was watching

Picked Out of a Catalog

by Anita Blackwell Robertson

"If you go to Oral Roberts University, I won't pay one penny for tuition."

My daddy did not care for Oral Roberts. He didn't know Mr. Roberts personally, but my mother did. She grew up in the same tiny communities he did outside Ada, Oklahoma, in the 1920s and 30s. Rural folks in these communities of Center and Egypt were mostly sharecroppers. Oral's dad was a "sometimes preacher" in the area, and Mom heard him speak occasionally.

She enjoyed Oral's sermons and often turned on his TV program as we were preparing for church on Sunday mornings. Mom was very religious. Dad, umm ... not so much. He objected to Rev. Roberts, considering him a charlatan.

One Sunday morning as I sat at the breakfast table buttering my toast, I heard on his program that he had opened a new university the previous fall in Tulsa. It was early 1966, and I was in my sophomore year at East Central State College in Ada. Living at home for the last two years while I went to school and worked part-time at J. C. Penney's was wearing thin. I was chomping at the bits, as Mom would say, to leave home and see what it was like to be on my own.

So, I sent for a catalog and application. It was a couple of weeks later after I received an acceptance letter from ORU, that my dad told me I was on my own financially if I went to "that school."

"You'll have to sell you're your little red Pontiac Tempest (which he had just given me and knew I loved), because I won't pay for your insurance or gasoline. You'll have to get a job or scholarships." He was adamant. Convinced that his only daughter was making an irreparable mistake by leaving a state college to attend a Bible school that wasn't even accredited, he thought I would change my mind once my funds were cut off.

He was wrong.

I received an academic scholarship, a work scholarship, and a grant. And I sold my precious car so I would have money for books and incidentals. Flapping my wings, I was ready to leap out of the nest to see if I could fly.

Devouring the school catalog, I was eager to find out all I could about my new university. Something about being a pioneer resonated with me, and I regretted I had not heard of ORU in time to be a part of that first-year class of 300 students.

The buildings were unlike any college campus I had ever seen, certainly not the staid, classic edifices at East Central. I studied all the catalog's photos so I might recognize some of the students when I got on campus. A dark-haired young man caught my attention. One of the pictures identified him as Al Robertson, and I resolved to look him up when I got there.

That fall after I settled in, I began my search for Mr. Robertson. Someone told me that he had been drafted during the summer. The Viet Nam conflict was in full swing. Draft notices were a fact of life for young men.

A few months into the fall semester, Al visited his friends one last time before shipping out for Advanced Individual Training (AIT) and then on to Viet Nam. In a serendipitous moment, I spotted him in uniform across the cafeteria at noon. A snippet of a song from South Pacific flashed through my mind: *"You may see a stranger across a crowded room. And somehow you know, you know even then that somewhere you'll see him again and again."* But what was I going to do? Run up to him and say, “Hi Al. I have a crush on you from your picture in the catalog?”

I had to let him go. After all, I was there for an education.

***

My dad was wrong about ORU’s being a Bible school. Sure, it had a college of theology, but it had been created to be a liberal arts university, and it offered majors in many areas. It was Oral Roberts University, after all. At East Central, I had declared an English major with the goal of becoming a teacher. That’s what my mother had dreamed of for herself and strongly encouraged me to do. Although I loved the subject, I couldn’t see myself in a classroom for the rest of my life. It never dawned on me that I could do many things with an English degree other than teach.

But I made an about-face at ORU and changed my major to performing arts. Introduced to the stage in my junior year of high school, applause became my siren song. The Performing Arts Department consisted of one professor. He moved from his native New York to be a different kind of pioneer at ORU, and we early students helped him build the department. He took me on as a special project to obliterate my Okie accent.

I relished, not only acting, but learning all aspects of a production: directing, costuming, lighting, props, scenery, advertising. I had completed most of my required subjects at East Central, so my two years at ORU were filled with learning the art of the "Theatuh." Those two years were like riding on a zip line—they ended too quickly.

I completed all my course work by the end of the 1968 spring semester. In order to graduate, the only thing I lacked was my senior paper. I really did not want to graduate and go out into the world, so I couldn't get motivated to write it. Therefore, I did not participate in ORU's first graduating class in 1968.

My work scholarship was in the Admissions Department as clerical support for Admissions Counselors. They traveled to schools and accompanied Oral on his crusades to speak to prospective students about coming to ORU. As I came to end of my studies, the director offered *me* a position as an Admissions Counselor. I accepted even though I hadn't graduated. I figured I would finish my paper over the summer and walk with the Class of 1969.

It didn't happen.

I couldn't imagine then what a drastic change my life would undergo before the Class of 1970 graduated.

***

One Sunday morning in late June 1968, I sat in the choir of Evangelistic Temple in Tulsa waiting for service to begin.

As my gaze swept over the congregation, I looked toward the back of the sanctuary and saw a raven-haired, gorgeous young man with military bearing dressed in a black turtleneck shirt and pants and a gold blazer.

Al Robertson—back from the war!

I began plotting how our paths might accidentally cross after waiting two years to meet him. Fortunately, Oral Roberts' son Richard solved my dilemma. Richard and I had previously met through a drama department event, and we both worked in the same building on campus. He, Al, and two other guys were renting an apartment together because there were no classes at ORU from June through August. They all worked during the summer.

One day, Richard invited several of his friends to his parents' home for a swim party. I happened to be one of those friends—and so did Al. The first time Al and I officially met, I was in a black swimsuit, and my figure had reached the zenith of its career: 38-24-36. I would never look that good again. It couldn't have been planned more meticulously if God had arranged it Himself.

Things progressed quickly after that "chance" encounter. Right away—July 27, 1968, to be specific—Al asked me out on our first date. Five months later to the day on December 27, 1968, we were married in

Evangelistic Temple's sanctuary.

Our wedding day was mostly a disaster. After something that can only happen in Oklahoma—an absolutely perfect December day of 72 degrees—a freak Arctic front moved in during the late afternoon, bringing with it a blizzard. At 5:00 p.m. it started snowing, and by our 8:00 ceremony, it was a white-out. Only Al's in-town relatives were able to attend. His mom and dad, who lived an hour away, could not get to their baby's wedding.

My dad had to be at work the next morning, so there was no chance he and Mom could spend the night in Tulsa. He was a mail carrier and his substitute was sick with the flu. My dad had it too and struggled to walk me down the aisle. But that was my dad for you. He was going to be there for his only daughter's wedding come Hell or high snow. He and my Ada relatives, who arrived in Tulsa before the storm, had to inch their way home in the ice and snow. A two-and-a-half-hour trip became five. Al and I couldn't even get out of town for our honeymoon 90 miles away in Oklahoma City.

But even with the inauspicious beginning and all the obstructions we encountered over the next half century, on December 27, 2018, we renewed our fiftieth wedding anniversary vows in the same church sanctuary, with the same minister, the same best man, the same maid of honor and the same singer.

ABOUT PAULA PETTIT SKENDER

Paula Pettit Skender comes to the writing field after two career choices: the armed forces and teaching.

During the Viet Nam War, while attending East Central

University (ECU) in Ada, Oklahoma, Paula decided to enlist in the local U.S. Army Reserves. This helped fund her transportation to school. Upon completing her Bachelor of Education degree, she chose to enter the military instead.

She worked ten years in the U.S. Army Adjutant General Corps. Signing for the commander, she wrote and edited all outgoing correspondence for the several commands assigned. Germany became one of those duty stations. Tasked with many outlier activities, she justified local ATMs, since German banks provided none. Separating from service as a captain with experience in piloting an airplane, firing a tank, shooting several firearms, such as a LAW, M14, M16, M60, she also achieved identification as a sharpshooter. She served as a safety officer on rifle ranges and won first place in manual of arms for rifle competition.

With five children, ages ten and below, she left the military and completed her Master of Education. Her studies advanced further into the doctorate program of Education Specialist in Curriculum and Instruction (EdS). She spent a quarter of a century as a teacher, immersed in reading, writing, math, science, and social studies. Her skill as an instructor focused on using the students' oral stories and applying them to the written word.

Paula became and Ada Writers' member in 2015, serving

as secretary. She participates in the Oklahoma Writer's Federation, Inc, and the Oklahoma Romance Writers Guild. She acts as leader for another group, Writing for Fun.

Under her given name, Paula authors nonfiction which includes true family tales and retelling Bible histories.

Paula's website www.networkofsilver.com introduces her, her family, and her stories

Returning Home

by Paula Pettit Skender

At the end of the Gulf war in May 1991, I returned to Oklahoma from Germany. While in the military, we moved to Oklahoma, Texas, Louisiana, and twice to Germany. However, with the constant experience of moving, it forced me to decide—my children needed a stable home.

Before this time, my children's life resembled traveling gypsies while their parents completed military assignments. Their childhood with its changing locations, friends, day care centers, and schools significantly differed from mine. I lived in the same old farmhouse until I was twenty, and Mom never worked outside the home.

Arriving at the home place where I grew up, I saw only a trailer house. The childhood shelter I remembered burned down in 1982 during my assignment at Fort Hood, Texas.

Mom and Dad chose not to replace their residence in the same spot. By the time it burned, the dirt road where I once ran barefoot on gravel was also gone. It changed to a major highway. Due to the busy traffic, my parents elected to build their new dwelling far behind the original location—on the back forty.

My five children and I temporarily moved into that trailer on the same spot where I lived as a child. However, I sought a different place away from heavy traffic. I also needed a location farther from Mom's place. If not, my kids would visit her too often.

I finally found a beautiful dwelling within four miles of Mom and Dad's. To my preference, no highway lay nearby. A gravel road welcomed me. The sale price sat far above my price range. But the house was close to family. It certainly looked like a lovely abode. It stood with a chimney that covered one whole wall. I offered a bid as high as I could go—which wasn't high. It was immediately turned down.

As I left that day after viewing the house—and after the turndown—I knew in a peculiar way that the house was mine. The turndown was only a delay. Of course, I've been wrong before, so I talked to the Lord and told Him if it proved to be mine, the real estate agent would have to call me back. I wasn't going to bid higher. My low bid would have to be accepted. There was no other way.

Within thirty days I received a phone call at work from that realtor. She agreed that I could have the large house and the fifteen acres without a problem even with my low bid. I knew this was a blessing from the Lord.

However, even though I knew the house was mine before her call—and although I talked it over with the Lord for my children's home—I still questioned why the low bid was accepted so easily for such a beautiful lodging. Small clues would follow. Actually, a hint shimmered within my sight the first day I viewed the house. I simply ignored it as a warning.

On that first day when I entered the house with the real estate agent—even before my bid—I went into each room looking at the spacious areas. When I walked into the master bedroom and entered the master bath, I jumped. A man stood against the left wall. I saw him from my peripheral vision. I quickly turned toward him. He wasn't there.

I simply considered I imagined his presence.

Two months of living in the spacious house proved delightful for my five children. No odd visions appeared in the master bath. The bedrooms fit our needs. Two baths seemed like heaven.

My sisters, Leslie and Rhonda, came by to check out my

new residence. I wasn't home. But as always, the door to my house stood unlocked in those days just like the doors to Mom and Dad's when they were gone. My sisters decided to tour without me. They walked through. Leslie entered the master bath and jumped at the sight of a man to her left. But since he disappeared, she reasoned she only imagined it.

She knew nothing about my own experience at the same spot.

As Rhonda and Leslie started to leave my house that day, they paused while talking in the dining room. Suddenly, the plastic cover over the air conditioner sprung straight forward three feet and tapped Rhonda on the back.

Rhonda straightened and looked around. Leslie, who faced the air conditioner, considered this peculiar. The trajectory looked intentional as though someone threw it forward. They tried to duplicate the spring-forward action of the cover. They tried several times to match the trajectory, but the cover would fall straight to the floor.

The air conditioner came from the original owner who was an old rodeo friend from Rhonda's teen days. When purchasing the house, I knew none of this background. I never met him. And I didn't know my sister knew him. He died in an auto accident in '91 and now an air conditioner he installed in the house he designed—the house I lived in—appeared to signal for Rhonda's attention.

Later, when Rhonda explained the incident of the flying air conditioner cover, I casually mentioned another odd experience in the master bath. Leslie surprised me with her nod of agreement as I spoke. She told me exactly where the man stood on the left side of the entrance.

A month later, my youngest daughter, Anna Lisa, age five at the time, started sleeping the night with me.

All the house lay quiet and I started to doze when she asked, "Mama, why is that man looking around the door?"

It was the door to the master bath. I told her simply. "No one is there, Anna Lisa."

Whatever this possible presence—a demon, or a figment of one's imagination—it's gone now after years of prayer. And yes, I still live in the beautiful, now old, house after twenty-five years.

SPECIAL NOTE: I do not believe there are ghosts. But I do believe there are demons that hang around after the human they harassed or controlled in this lifetime has passed. They might even try to imitate the appearance of the person they troubled in an attempt to fool gullible loved ones. I speculate, of course. I do not know. However, some people have said they've seen their deceased loved one after their death. I know this could not be.

In Ecclesiastes 9:5 the Bible says the dead know nothing. From other Biblical texts our spirits do not walk the earth after death because as I told a dear cousin before her death, ". . . absent from the body, present with the Lord" II Corinthians 5:8 (KJV).

However, Scripture indicates from its stories that demons probably look for a new warm body once they are forced to vacate the body they harassed or no longer can reside in—like Legion (many demons) who begged Jesus to enter the swine (a warm body) after they were forced out of the man (Matthew 8:28-34, Mark 5:1-20, Luke 8:26-39, KJV).

Leisel

by Paula Pettit Skender

Leisel, Germany lay midway between our two duty stations when a house opened there for lease. This allowed us to bring our two toddlers overseas to join us while we served in the military.

The only bath in the Leisel house lay in an eerie basement. To reach it, one walked a long dark hallway with rough stone walls that looked like centuries-old dungeon fortifications. It may have been. The town appears in historical documents as early as 1180 A.D.

Before our toddlers arrived, I felt a threat from the dank, dark stone hallway that led to the only bathroom in that three-story house. I felt someone wanted to stab me. I shook it off as nonsense. But when our children arrived, the screaming began.

The first time I took our toddlers to their bath, Jim, the three-year-old started screaming before I placed one foot down on the first steep step to the dungeon. He grabbed and clung to my legs shrieking. Elizabeth grabbed my neck and howled as I carried her down the shadowed steps.

Our toddlers' reaction to the dungeon trudge lasted during our stay there. I kept quiet about my own feelings and attempted to act as though everything was normal. Now I realize I never spoke to my husband about the strangeness at Leisel.

On-base housing opened three months later. We moved immediately. My husband had to drive an hour one-way daily to work.

My duty as Adjutant of Baumholder military base felt much better. I lived a few blocks from my office. I could walk to work. My husband served as Commander at that remote signal corps site. Life was good. Leisel forgotten.

The summer before we left Germany, as was routine, my husband played softball with the boys, and I sat on a pallet beside a woman named Patterson. I didn't know her, but she was talking about this house she lived in and how her husband woke up in the middle of the night. Lightning flashed overhead. A man stood over his bed with a long knife. She then mentioned, "That house has only one bathroom in that horrible basement."

Her words reminded me of Leisel. I wondered if

Germans always built their baths in the basement. "Where do you live?"

"Leisel. Your husband offered us the rest of the lease to stay there. We weren't even required to repay him the five-hundred dollars to refill the oil heater."

I knew nothing about my husband's generosity. But it appeared he wanted to leave Leisel, also. After the ballgame, I told him Mrs. Patterson's story.

His response came slow and guarded. "I walked down dungeon hall one day. An old man appeared there dressed in clothing from another time. He carried a long knife in one hand."

"Didn't you confront him . . . speak to him?"

"No. I walked on by as though he wasn't there . . . because I don't think he was."

Photo provided by author

ABOUT D.W. SMITH

D.W. (Doyle) Smith began writing by keeping a notebook handy as a young man. Over the many years, a considerable stack of "stuff" accumulated.

His first published work at seventy-four was a short story collection, *Tales From Rattlesnake Gulch,* 2017. Followed by *My, My,* 2018, another short story collection. His first novel, *Gold, Ghosts, and Woollys*, was published in 2019. *James*, a science-fiction novel, is due for publication in 2020 as is *Homer*, another novel.

Doyle, now older than dirt, stays active doing church and community service and taking long walks in the desert near San Antonio, New Mexico. Yes, there is a San Antonio, New Mexico. It's near Rattlesnake Gulch where Doyle, a transplanted Okie, now lives and writes.

Chickens

by D. W. Smith

I suppose I should confess my sin and repent. But I'm in a dilemma. I don't know exactly how to confess my sin. I didn't intend to commit this sin. I just opened my mouth and inserted my foot, that's all.

Now, as a good number of folks know, I live on Rattlesnake Gulch. That's out in central New Mexico. You'll not find it on no map. I named the place. I've already told my saga of how I got here, and why, for obvious reasons, I named this place Rattlesnake Gulch.

A little background might help here. I'm an Independent Baptist. I read my authorized King James Bible a lot and have for many years. I have read my Bible enough over many, many years, to know what it says and where it says it. Now, that does not mean I understand all I read. I must confess, I don't. As a matter of fact, several pastors I've known have accused me of being a slow steady. At least slow steady is one of the nicer names they've used.

I'm not apologizing here. I attend and support my church and have for many years because that's the right thing for me to do. Amen. But here's where things go downhill to hell in a hand basket! I was talking out loud—or maybe thinking out loud—when I should have paid attention to who was listening to my rhetoric.

In my little community on the bare edge of civilization, there is one little store. It's all we got. It has the necessities of life. Donuts, soda pop, bacon, eggs, donuts, gasoline, donuts, oh, and donuts, and ice cream too. Now, that's chocolate donuts and chocolate ice cream. I may be a little weak in faith, or is that willpower? Donuts are the epitome of sin. I know. I have indulged in that forbidden pastry more than once and been ousted out of several sizes of trousers. Now you tell me that's not a high price to pay for one little transgression!

I know all the people down at that little store that sell those donuts and ice cream, and I guess they know me. All those nice folks live in our little community. So does the neighborhood chicken!

Now, this old Dominicker rooster showed up down at our store some time ago and took up residence. No one seemed to know where that old rooster came from, nor did anyone seem to care. Maybe he came on a flying saucer. Out here, every now and then, we get overrun with flying saucers. Anyway, the rooster shows up and gets to be an item in no time. From somewhere, chicken feed and water soon appear by the door of the store. The compassionate people take pity on the poor rooster and share their potato chips and popcorn with the rooster. I even gave that old rooster a bite of my donut. He didn't get no chocolate; I saw to that.

As we all know, I'm a transplanted Okie, and I have a real soft spot in my heart—or maybe a soft spot in my head—for a rooster.

I had a real prize rooster back in Oklahoma. Rojo by name. "The terror of Pontotoc County." People would sit out in their car and honk their horn. "Where's your rooster?" they would demand.

Rojo, I guess, thought he was a bad dog or something. That chicken would fight at the drop of a word. That rascal had never in his whole miserable life heard or earned one kind word. I even tried to think of something good to say about that rooster. I couldn't think of anything. Well, maybe how would he taste fried.

This ain't about Rojo. That's ancient history. I've lived out here some nine years now, and sometimes, I kinda missed my old chicken in Oklahoma, “The terror of Pontotoc County.”

My church is near our one and only store with its resident rooster. That chicken, more than once, has been the topic of conversation for the community for quite some time.

Some of us are standing out in front of our little church when the rooster takes a little stroll out in full view. All I said was, “If I still stole chickens, I’d nab that rooster.”

I swear I ain’t never stole a chicken in my life. I don’t think I ever saw one worth stealing. I don’t even like buffalo wings. I eat nuggets occasionally.

All I was doing was making amusing conversation. Nor was I paying the least bit of attention to who was listening to my amusing comments.

I kinda feel sorry for anyone that does not have a church family. If you don’t have a church family, you don’t go to church much. And like any good family, some members of a family will overstep the merits of common sense for what they decide is a worthy cause.

The neighborhood chicken is doing well and has gained a large degree of notoriety and respect. The community comes to the aid of the chicken. Somebody, out of the goodness of their heart, provides the neighborhood chicken with a used doghouse to sleep in. Being an old, transplanted Okie, I knew that would never work. The chicken didn't sleep *in* the doghouse. He roosted on top of it.

All remained well in my uncomplicated world for three days after my careless choice of amusing words.

Now, I'm minding my business out on Rattlesnake Gulch. That's mostly looking out the window for rattlers crawling across my dirt or maybe a cow, rabbit, Javalina, or a lizard out in the distance.

Anyway, a car shows up in my driveway. There's this woman and her kid I've tormented since she was in diapers.

"We brought you a rooster," says the kid, beaming from ear to ear. "Now you won't need to steal the one down at the store."

Now these are the same people that took up a collection and bought me a cell phone for a Christmas present. When I didn't carry that cell phone, I was accused of being ungrateful. Now I got a chicken! And you just can't tell a smiling kid and her mother you don't want a chicken.

Since my wife died a couple of years ago, I haven't had anything on the place that eats except me. Nor have I had to clean up after anything. Now I got a rooster that eats better than I do. He beds down on the handrail around my porch; he leaves his natural deposits all over; and he has a tendency to start crowing about three in the morning. A loudmouth rooster, crowing at three in the morning, resurrects the dead.

The dilemma I face now is obvious. It's chicken trouble. Is it ungrateful me or the inconsiderate rooster that's creating the trouble?

Fix 'er Up

by D.W. Smith

Now I don't want to appear unreasonable, naïve, or downright hardheaded, but that woman just don't get it! She don't like my fine brown truck! Me and my truck are offended!

Now, I got a recent responsibility to defend my truck. We've been an item since 1974. The fact that me and my truck, against overwhelming odds, have made it well into the 21st century is beside the point.

Back in 1974, I was driving down the road in my other old truck; it was really old and really ugly. Anyway, I see this beat up, sort of new truck sitting out front of a used car lot with a sign on the windshield, "make offer."

Now, I had known that used car dealer several years. "Jerry," I says, "What's wrong with that truck?"

"It's got a cough," says Jerry.

"Trucks don't catch cold," I said.

"That one did," said Jerry. "It sneezes too. For you, it's a real fixer upper. Cheap too. I'll make you a deal."

"You've made me a deal before with that last piece of junk. I owe you," I said.

"Here's your chance to get even. This one's a bargain. You can have it running like a top in no time. Besides, it's only four years old. Of course, you'll need to do something with the cough. The–farmer that traded it to me said the cough didn't amount to much," said Jerry.

Against my better judgment, I said, "Let me hear that cough."

"Here's the keys," said Jerry. "Take her for a spin. Don't go too far. Ain't got much gas in it!"

"You're trying to sell me a bill of goods, ain't you?" I asked.

"Nah, for you it's a bargain," said Jerry.

"Jerry, that's a farm truck. Some farmer has used it up. Look at all them dents," I said.

"It gives it character," said Jerry. "No charge for cow dents. You can fix those. You'll have that truck good as new in just no time."

"Give me the keys," I said.

Whoof – whoof – whoof… Rev it up… Whoof – whoof – whoof…

"Jerry, I wouldn't trust that thing to make it the six blocks to my garage. It's sick."

"It just got a little cough, that's all," said Jerry. "Besides, you ain't seen the best part."

"And just what's its best part?" I demanded.

"The back bumper," said Jerry. "It'll make you a fine tow truck for that race car you got. You can go racing in style. You'll see. Look at that bumper. It calls to you!"

"How much for the bumper?" I asked.

"Not much," said Jerry. "I'll throw in the truck."

That was 1974. The bumper has never needed repair. The truck has needed more attention than my wives over the last 45 years

Now I don't intend to make an issue out of this, but since 1974, I've had three wives, and I've been single for the last year and a half. The one thing all three of my wives agreed upon was that my fine brown truck was not fit for anything except me.

It seems they were offended by the holes in the floorboard and the dirt in the seat. Neither of which bothers me.

The new woman in my life seems to agree with my dead wives, that my "fine brown truck" ain't fit for women to ride around in. The way she said I was a real gentleman because I opened the door for her just didn't come out right. So, what if the doors are a little hard to open? I know how to "bump 'em," and those holes in the floorboard are good for ventilation, and the dirt is clean dirt.

I've had that truck a lot longer than I've had wives. I sure as hell didn't plan on it that way. On top of that, my radio don't work!

Here's the high points. When my oldest son was about 16, he borrowed my truck to go girling. Anyway, he killed my radio. "Son," I says, "you aim to fix my radio?"

"Sure, pop," he says.

I've been waiting 40 years, and he ain't fixed my radio yet. Maybe, that's why women don't want to ride in my truck. The radio don't work!

My three sons are waiting for me to die to see who gets my truck. They all learned to drive in my fine brown truck. Maybe, I'll just be buried in my truck. Maybe, I'll just quit "fixin' `er up." That'll teach them boys and the women in my life, too.

Gratitude

by D.W. Smith

You think you got trouble? Try this on for size:

I got a big ugly black bull laying on my front porch! It's not much of porch, but it's all I got, and I want him off my porch. You can't just shoo a bull off the porch like a chicken.

I suppose I should explain some stuff here. Here's a situation: I have the deed to a postage-stamp-size piece of dirt here on Rattlesnake Gulch. That's out in the middle of thousands of acres of BLM land (Bureau of Land Management). I bought the place from a man that lived here 27 years. He built the place.

You get the gist. Lots of strange things goes on out here that nobody has a good explanation for. There are UFO sightings, aliens walking about, woolly boogers, and things that just don't make no sense to transplanted Okies from the sticks.

It seems I live in open-range country. Critters have the

right-of-way. If you don't want livestock in your yard, you build a fence on your place and lock the gate with no trespassing signs.

Here's something! Cows can't read! And anybody that knows anything about cows knows they would rather tear down the fence as go through an open gate.

Here's something else. The herd bull likes my porch! Not only does the bull like my front porch, but he likes my daughter's back porch, too. My daughter has a little house out back; the bull likes her porch, too!

Now this isn't the first herd bull I've seen that wanted away from all those heifers. If you ain't been around livestock, I'm not going to explain. It ain't how much the bull eats that's important.

Then again, this is a strange bull. Maybe an alien brought him on a flying saucer. We'll just not go there now.

The other day a little before sun-up, I opened the front door of my house to see what my world looked like. I like sunrises and sunsets. Somehow, I just wasn't expecting bull on my porch at sunrise. Kinda catchy, don't you think?

I've come home to my little patch of dirt more than once to find a herd of cows in my yard. Cows eat shrubs and tree leaves. I guess it supplements their diet. There's not a blade of grass within 50 miles of where I live. Here on

Rattlesnake Gulch, cows eat what us old Okies call weeds. The rancher that owns the cows says there is several species of the "weed" the cows eat. Here's another tidbit: My cows in Oklahoma ate grass. Oh well, this is alien land, and I don't do cows anymore. I'm retired.

This neighborhood bull ain't the only strange cow I've seen out here. The nearest town of any size where I live is Socorro, New Mexico. When I go to town, I usually go down the back roads. There are farms along the Rio Grande River. Being a transplanted Okie that knows nothing about farming and livestock in New Mexico, I like seeing how the locals farm. I just never would make it as a farmer or rancher out here. I don't even know what they are doing, nor do I know anything about New Mexico cows.

They raise lots of cattle on those farms. At least most of the cows looks like Oklahoma cows, but there is an exception: Wattie by name.

My wife, now deceased, was an Okie too. But she didn't know nothing about cows; she was a city girl. Anyway, we were taking a leisurely drive down the back roads. There are cows on the winter pastures like Okie farmers have, but there is *this* cow.

"What is that? Is that a cow? Look at those horns," she said.

By now I'm hunting a place to park. I never seen no cow like that.

This cow has two horns every bit of three feet long that's growing straight out in front of her.

I know I've been accused of living in a vacuum sometimes. But I've been around cattle for 70 years, and I've never seen nothing like that! I got to know about this cow. We took pictures!

I had seen that cow several times. I looked for that cow every time I went by. I even made a special trip a time or two to show that cow to visitors from back home in Oklahoma.

The one thing they all agreed on: "I ain't seen no cow like that." They took pictures too!

One day on my way to town, I see this farmer seeing about his cattle. I stopped for a "howdy do." "That gray cow? Is that a cow?" I asked.

"That's a Wattie," said the man. "Had her 22 years; she's had 20 calves. She's a 'Watusie'."

"I've never seen one nor never heard of one," I said. "And I've never seen horns like that either. I've seen longhorns with big horns growing north and south, but I've never seen two horns pointing east."

"She's a looker," said the farmer. "You want a closer

look?"

"Is she as mean as she looks?" I asked.

"She's just a big ol' pet." The farmer got a sack of feed out of his truck and headed to a nearby trough. Here came that cow at a dead run with those horns looking like lances held by jousting knights.

While Wattie was after the cattle cubes, those horns were just everywhere. When she was pasture grazing, those big horns nearly gouged the dirt. I was impressed with Wattie.

Now, I got this porch setter. I call him Uffie—short for UFO. No that's ULB, unidentified laying bull.

"Get off my porch, bull," I demand. "You git!"

After getting to his feet, he deposits a nice cow patty on my porch. If that ain't gratitude.

It's a good thing my wife is already dead. A bull on her porch would have done her in!

Miss Mims

by D.W. Smith

I'm going to tell this tale as best I can remember. The year was 1948. I was a six-year-old that was about to start school that fall. C-Bar wasn't any place in 1948, nor is C-Bar any place now. It's plowed ground with the gas well where the playground used to be.

C-Bar is where I started to school. It was one room—let's call it a classroom—with a closet for books, supplies, winter coats, and detention. Yes, detention. Better known in my world as Miss Mims' Jail. That was just no place you wanted to go! I have been indicted, convicted, and served time in Mims' Jail more than once!

Miss Mims ran the place. Miss Mims had run the place since time began! Most certainly since the flood. You know, the Noah story about the flood. There were those that swore Miss Mims was either Noah's wife or maybe one of his sons' wives. I'm just repeating hearsay now!

C-Bar is where my mama started the first grade. Miss Mims was warden according to my mother. My mother was tough! She served eight years in detention. My mama's explanation.

Let me draw a little mental picture. Here it's my first day in the first grade. Miss Mims is setting at her desk. She leans forward and looks over her glasses. "I knew your mother!" Her beady little eyes penetrate down to my bladder. I want to tinkle on the flames of hell! I discover I am not dead, and a cold chill runs up my spine to the back of my neck. It makes my hair stand on end! To add to my misery, I want to run or cry, but I am afraid to.

Miss Mims never takes her beady eyes off me. She is still leaning forward, looking over her glasses. She raises her hands. One finger points at me and slowly drifts, "That was your mother's desk in her first grade. Will it do for you?"

"Uh huh," I whisper shaking in my new shoes.

"That is, 'yes ma'am,' to you," said Miss Mims, not taking her beady eyes off me.

"Yess `um," I said.

"Yes ma'am," said Miss Mims.

"Yes ma'am," I said.

"We have rules," said Miss Mims.

"Yess um," I said.

“Yes ma’am,” said Miss Mims in a slow clear voice. “We have rules.”

“Yess `um, uh, yes ma’am,” I managed to say.

That tone of Miss Mims’ voice resonated from the very depths of hell, I was certain! Later, I knew without the slightest doubt. That tone came from capital H-E-L-L!

I got a pretty fair understanding of hell down at Long Prairie church. Old Ellis could suspend a whole congregation over hell’s fire, clutching at a strand of a spider’s web!

Miss Mims had a man. According to my mama, no one—absolutely no one—dared to ask who he was, where he came from, what his name was, or what his connection was to Miss Mims. The story goes, during the summer of ‘35 or maybe ‘36, he showed up on the premises of C-Bar. All anyone knew was he was Miss Mims’ man.

Miss Mims had been schoolmarm since the Stone Age. No one I ever knew could remember when Miss Mims came to C-Bar. My mama said she didn’t know. My grandpa bought that half section of Indian land at C-Bar sometime in late 20s, and Miss Mims was the schoolmarm then and had been schoolmarm at C-Bar since—I guess forever.

All anyone had to say about C-Bar School was Miss

Mims ran the school, and you'd get an education—whether you wanted it or not! As far as anyone around C-Bar knew, Miss Mims' word was law. Some survivors of Mims' school went on to high school somewhere. A few, so they say, even went to college much later on.

Now here's a fact: I never seen nor heard tell of anyone that's spent one minute in the presence of Miss Mims at C-Bar that didn't remember it.

C-Bar school closed its doors forever at the end of school year the spring of 1949.

In the fall of 1949 was an obituary for Miss Mims, longtime resident of C-Bar. She passed away at her home on C-Bar school property. She was survived by 783 children she knew by name. Many of those children became successful adults, well-prepared for the world outside of C-Bar.

Oldageitus

by Doyle Smith

The first time I was made aware of *oldageitus* has to be at least 65 years ago. If you can remember anything that happened 65 years ago, you probably got a dose of it.

I'm obviously dating myself. I still remember—or I think I remember—back 65 years ago. My God, I was already half growed.

My grandpa was in his 70s out on the farm, still plowing with a team of horses. As usual, I was around under his feet, mostly getting in the way. Grandpa had been known to lead me down the garden path now and then. I was about to take a little stroll.

"I got the sickness coming on me," said Pa.

"You need a doctor or something?" I asked concerned.

"Won't help none," said Pa. "Too far gone."

"Well what's ailing ye?" I asked.

"Oldageitus," said Pa

."What's that?" I asked. "I ain't heard about no sickness like that."

"It's catchin'," said Pa. "I gots it. It's been coming on me for quite some time."

"Don't you need to see old Doc Adams?" I ask.

"Won't help. He's down with it, too," said Pa. "Ain't no cure for it."

"How's you know you got it?' I asked.

"Gots all the symptoms," said Pa. "I'd soon walk 100 yards and go through the gate as to step over a knee-high picket fence. That's how's you knows you gots it. Now, I got it! Took me a long time to get it, but I got it now."

It seems to me, sixty years later, that I got oldageitus. I'm having to make several new adjustments in my life. Could it possibly be my attitude? I'm here to tell you, I'm not dead yet! I'm quite well aware I should be, but I'm not dead yet! I'm protesting now.

Recently, I found myself in the local hospital. From time to time, it seems people like me are required to go to the hospital. I guess it was my turn. Anyway, there I lay, plugged up to the wall, to the juice bottles, and told, "Don't get up."

"What happens when my eyeball starts floating?" I asked.

"Call a nurse," she said.

"Well, I can go myself," I said. "Been doing it for 75 years, mostly without help."

"We need to measure your urine," she said.

"And just how are you going to measure my end?" I asked.

"Urine," she said.

"My end?" I demanded. "How you aim to measure my end?"

"No," she said, "Urine. You know, when you tinkle."

"Well, I didn't know I pinkled either," I said. "I don't pinkle. I pee, and I need to now."

"I'll get you a urinal," she said.

"I don't need young Nell. I need a pee pot, and I need it now!" I said.

"Do I need to help you?" she asked.

"Not at my age!" I said. "Maybe less medication and my hearing aids would help."

It had been so long since I had been in the hospital or even been sick. I didn't have a doctor or primary care physician they said I needed for a follow-up visit. Someone agreed to take me on.

At my age we take what we can get. Being a transplanted Okie in a foreign land, the concept that poor people have poor ways always makes perfect sense to me. I don't think it applies out here in the desert.

They tell me there's a show on TV about a 14-year-old surgeon. I never saw the show. Heard about it. Don't believe it. But then, my new lady doctor can't be a day over 18. Oh well.

Now this new doctor is a pretty young girl. That's what I see, anyway. She's "cute as a bug's ear" and as young as my granddaughter that's a registered nurse. I know what I see! I got lens implants in my eyes, and I know what I hear when I have my hearing aids plugged in my ears. We'll just not go into any other of my mechanical aids. Remember I'm pushing 80!

Anyway, the young lass typed all my latest vital statistics in her machine, and then she began to explain what she is recording on the computer screen. That machine knows about every case of hiccups I've had for the last 20 years—three states away!

That's when it dawned on me that machine knew all the details about my prostate, hemorrhoids, and the garden hose up my hiney ten years ago. And now this young girl is trying to explain old age to me. Not only that, but she's saying words I ain't never heard and I don't understand.

There's more to my troubles. Read on. When I got out of

the hospital, some cutie-pie doctor in earshot of my church pastor told me I couldn't go home and stay alone for a few days. My pastor told my cutie-pie doctor he'd get someone to stay in my spare bedroom and see that I stay alive. The doctor said that's agreeable or I could stay in the hospital. I swear I don't remember all the details of this arrangement.

After all, when your pastor and your doctor get a plan, what could possibly go wrong? I've not had a wife to give me orders in a couple years. When they let me out—or maybe threw me out—of the hospital, my pastor provided me transportation back to my home.

"Several of the ladies in church offered to see to your needs," the pastor said.

"I didn't know I had needs," I said. "I can fend for myself."

"No, you can't," the pastor said. "You're getting help. The doctor said so."

"I don't need help," I said.

"You're getting help," the pastor said. "The doctor said so. The church ladies said so. And Vee said so."

"What's Vee got to do with this?" I demanded. "She's not married."

"She will be soon. Everybody knows that," said my smiling pastor. "Vee will be providing aid and comfort for the needy. Everybody knows you need all the help you can get!"

Maybe I do need help.

Porch Killer

by D.W. Smith

The bats are out!

Where I came from in southeastern Oklahoma, the bats came out after dark. It was an expression in common use to describe all kinds of day-to-day insanity. In Hicksville, I didn't have to explain, "the bats are out."

But then, I moved. Out here on Rattlesnake Gulch, the bats will make an appearance in the daytime. We had just moved here on Rattlesnake Gulch. It's the middle of July, it's hotter than blazes, the screen door provides ventilation—we think—and the bat arrives and attaches itself to the screen door.

The second day here, I had to deal with a rattler on my porch or get a new wife. Now here's the thing about letting sleeping dogs lie. (Is that like in lying hound dogs?) Here's one for you. How do you wake a sleeping rattler? Okay, how about shoo a bat off your screen door?

Within a week, I knew this was not Oklahoma. The rattler was easy enough to deal with. That is, what was left of him. My little wife dealt with the snake on her own terms. She blasted that sucker with the shotgun. Neither the snake or the porch survived. She killed both of them.

I just got the porch repaired when the bat showed up. I outran her to the shotgun! Within a week, my attitude on gun control had changed. I'm just not too sure about teaching a woman how to use the shotgun. I knew from experience the screen door was about to vanish.

Here is another dilemma. Try telling a seventy-year-old wife with a shotgun in her hand not to kill the porch. "Shoo the snake off the porch, then blast him!"

There are times when it's easier not to give instructions to your wife. Don't ask me what kind of bat lights on your screen door in the middle of the day. I can tell you it's a bat. The bat has a death wish around my little wife. It seems she has a thing about bats.

She has a thing about rattlers too, but bats are vampires about to suck the blood out of a living soul. I've heard mention of bad omens and ghosts, too.

I'd heard such stories back in the hills. Lord help if a bat showed up at a funeral. I've heard it was a soul not wanting to leave.

This much I knew for sure, nobody I knew would be caught dead around the cemetery after dark. The bats would get you. I don't know if that applies out here where the bats come out in the daytime.

My little wife is of the opinion that a good snake is a dead snake. My explaining to her with a shotgun in her hand that there are good snakes and bad snakes is like pouring water on a duck's back. Any snake on the porch is a candidate for execution.

It's not so much the snake that concerns me; it's the porch. When I married that woman years ago, I didn't know she was a porch killer. Another one bit the dust

WHO ARE THE ADA WRITERS?

We are a group of writers of all ages and abilities, who enjoy telling stories. We write fiction and nonfiction, poetry, haiku, essays, memoirs, and biographies. Our meetings provide fun and support, as well as learning, literary briefings, and activities. Dedicated to our community, we offer writing competitions and workshops for all ages. Local schools in our area are included in the contests providing children the opportunity to win awards for their talents.

If you are interested in learning more or joining our group, send an email to adawriters.ok@gmail.com.

We would love to hear from you.

Made in the USA
Columbia, SC
30 September 2020

21729160R00196